simple happy essentials

Shout From The Rooftops In Your Stilettos

she
simple happy essentials

Shout From The Rooftops In Your Stilettos

Copyright © 2006 Julie Hunt
All rights reserved.

ISBN: 1-933596-74-0

SHE
An Imprint of Morgan James Publishing, LLC
1225 Franklin Ave Ste 325
Garden City, NY 11530-1693
U.S.A.
Or contact the author at:
http://www.shesite.com

layout editor: Artur Orlowski, e-mail: artur@orlowskiart.com;
copy editor: Kathleen Rake, e-mail: kathleen@thewriteway.ca;
cover design: Michael Ehlert, e-mail: info@blipstudios.com.

Bonus FREE Mentoring Program
Expand Your Stiletto Collection

Get your FREE personal guide to delightful stiletto fun and deep self-exploration.
Enjoy having a personal mentor by your side to remind, encourage, and uplift
you on this fabulous self-discovery journey.

Go to www.shesite.com or call 619-237-4917.

Access Code: epiphany

Begin Today!

Acknowledgments

My gratitude and thanks to:

Mom, thank you for a lifetime of lessons and examples – continually believing that the impossible is possible and dreams-do-come-true. Your words continually inspire me. And, you were right. Anything is possible!

Dad for your wit, wisdom, support, and encouragement. You are my rock in a limitless world that keeps "chuckin' to infinity." You and Jo Ann are the most brilliant role models of living by example. Thank you for creating a wonderfully safe space filled with unconditional love.

David W. Collier, my lover and soul mate. You are the 99% to my 1%. You rock my world in more ways than I can express. Everyday you inspire me to be a better human. Your vision for what is possible is magical and off-the-charts inspiring. I adore and love you... more than mochas, muffins, and mangos!

Great big love to my lifelong "matching blue velour shirt" friend and angel, Cassie Massie. No one has been on this journey with me longer than you have, and never for one millisecond did you stop believing in me or doubt my success. You remind me everyday to see the beauty, possibility, and gifts in every situation. Will you marry me?!

Michael Port who is my perfect role model for Thinking Big. You are pure abundance. Your energy, support, and love (but not in a weird way) is beyond extraordinary!

The wonderfully soft-spoken powerhouse and amazing woman, Kathleen Rake. You have profoundly affected this work – above all giving it your clear, clean, and clever touch. You make it feel more like magic than gibberish. Thank you for your wonderful spirit, editing genius, creative vision, and splashes of 'triple-shot-no-foam' fun!

My family, friends who are more than family, clients who were ever so patient and gracious with crazy deadlines, and every virtual expert who tossed everything else aside in the hour to help. I am so grateful and appreciative of your vision and talent.

There are so many others whose hard work have shaped and influenced my life. Some I know intimately and others I have only read or heard their work. I honor and celebrate each person for their courage – for they were the first to give voice to these profound beliefs and principles. They have given us a foundation to live more bold, brilliant, and authentic lives.

Most importantly, thanks to each and every woman who is traveling on this journey. I hope you see as much beauty inside of you as I see.

TABLE OF CONTENTS

VII

INTRODUCTION

You Are The Star And Leading Lady

Welcome! You just flung open the windows and many marvelous doors that lead to life's expansive balconies, rooftops, and playgrounds! Make this your place – your playground and safe haven. The place where you are free to be everything you've always wanted and more. A place that honors you.

Your heart is welcome here. Your truth is heard. You are understood and encouraged. Each step on your journey reveals the streaming technicolor version of your life. Let it fill the screen of your heart, mind, and body.

Look up… that's you… the leading lady. Stunning, happy, brilliant, authentic, and whole. You're strutting your stuff on rooftops, reaching for your pinnacle while wearing your saucy stilettos. You're living life… and living it large!

See the movie of your life as you want it to be. This space has been created just for you – a beautiful, safe, and serene environment that guides you and gives you the absolute go-ahead to reveal the many marvelous parts of you. Play and participate. Step into the shoes of the leading lady in this stunning Hollywood motion picture; the picture that is your life. The red carpet is rolled out for you. You are the star. It's a box office hit and it's showing off your brilliant life!

Feel the energy of your truth and many simple happy pleasures as you flow through this guide. Let the silly statements, inspiring quotes, exploratory exercises, quick-healing strategies, grounding rituals, rich dialogue, and revealing writings soak into your life. Feel a wonderful sense of freedom wash over you and see the unlimited possibility of truly loving your life!

Here's to girls everywhere who are about to step on to the red carpet! I'm celebrating the star-like qualities in you.

Happiness Comes From Within

Do you believe you have the power to shape your life and happiness... for good?

I do. Yes, I do!

Happiness spans the globe. It comes in more shapes, sizes, colors, forms, and funky fashions than you can imagine. Look around. There are splashes of it everywhere. Sometimes it's as simple as a clear blue sky or as grand as falling in love for the very first time. But no matter where you are looking or what you are feeling, true happiness always comes from within.

What if you never had to depend on people, places, or material things to spark to your smile?

The truest happiness you will ever experience comes when you have a mad passionate love affair with yourself. When you know who you are and what you want... when you accept all that you are and have a sense of peace knowing you do your best each and every day... this is the ultimate in happiness. The kind of internal happiness that can never, ever be taken away from you. It is true joy. It's pure pleasure – and the kind of happiness I know you can find.

I believe you have the power to shape your life and find complete happiness! That's you at center stage. Throw back the curtains of shame, guilt, anger, sadness, unworthiness, resentment, fear, tension, and fatigue. It's a show stopper! Joy, happiness, worthiness, self-love, well-being, and fulfillment fill the stage. The second you grab that mic you allow free-flowing joy to wash over your life – authentic and lasting happiness that comes from within. **Every bit of happiness and goodness you desire is right inside of you.**

On your mark. Get ready. Get set. Go!

During our time together, oodles of joyful information will stream into your heart, mind, spirit, and soul. Not only will you discover that warm, wonderful smile of yours, but you will *feeeeeeel* a deep sense of freedom – enjoying and appreciating each new day you are given.

In the most magical and wondrous way, *Shout From The Rooftops In Your Stilettos* will inspire and unlock the beauty within you. You will become more intimately (and lovingly) acquainted with yourself. Powerful benefits will begin to emerge. You will:

- Become very clear on what is truly important so you can relax and enjoy those aspects of your life.
- Be your own best friend and begin to pamper, care, and love yourself.
- Put the important things in perspective, have more fun, and eliminate many burdens of the past.
- Express yourself boldly and creatively without negative thought patterns sneaking in and ruining your party.
- Eliminate stress and overwhelm when you gain the strength and courage to say "No."
- Enjoy the present moment and stop fretting about the future.
- Change what you want to change in your life far easier than you ever did before.
- Learn to love yourself as a complete woman and live in a steady state of gratitude.
- Speak, sing, and shout positive statements about yourself.
- Love yourself first.

*"I have found that most people are about as happy
as they make up their minds to be."*

Abraham Lincoln

The Rule Is: There Are No Rules

I always imagined *Shout From The Rooftops In Your Stilettos* would read like a juicy novel. You would connect immediately with the main character, fall in love with her… and she would be you!! But as this marvelous little film (*Shout From The Rooftops In Your Stilettos*) played out, it turned into something a little less 'novel-y' and a bit more 'pick me up and play.'

Shout From the Rooftops in Your Stilettos is a personal journey and an adventure for you to enjoy. Because it's your story – that really only means one thing to me: it's all love and no rules. So, you just go ahead and toss your book back and forth – front to back – start to finish – to and fro. Disregard all preconceived notions or rules you might have had. Set them aside for now.

Shout From The Rooftop In Your Stilettos is a stage designed especially for you to skip around on. Start from the back, the middle, or any ol' page that suits you. Close your eyes and flip to a random section to see what inspiration is waiting to jump off the pages and greet you – revealing itself to you – in that very moment of your life. Dive right in or tuck a page in your pocket for later. Scribble love notes in the margins or copy the page, and send it to friends. Let them witness and celebrate your light. The purpose here is to play, have fun, and feel free in flow.

With the "No Rules" philosophy, I gently give just a few suggestions and explanations that might make your life a little easier. Use this guide in whatever way works for you and let the powerful benefits of true happiness stream through your life quickly, clearly, easily, and lovingly.

> *"Our happiness depends on the habit of mind we cultivate.*
> *So practice happy thinking every day.*
> *Cultivate the merry heart, develop the happiness habit,*
> *and life will become a continual feast."*
>
> Norman Vincent Peale

How To Use This Guide

As promised, here are a few quick tips so you can easily navigate through this book and the accompanying electronic version.

Hyperlinks: You will find throughout the eBook version various hyperlinks that are <u>underlined</u>. Example: <u>www.shesite.com</u>. If you are connected to the internet, you can click the hyperlinks that begin with "www" and your internet browser will automatically open to that internet page. (If it does not automatically open – right click the mouse and click on "Open Hyperlink." You will be taken directly to that webpage.) To return to the eBook, simply close or minimize the online window of your web browser. If you only see text <u>underlined</u> without "www," it is a link within this guide that will skip you over to another related topic you may want to read, revisit, or reference.

Table of Contents: When you are in the Table of Contents section at the beginning of the book, you can click on any topic listed and be taken immediately to that section of the eBook.

Email Addresses: These work in a similar way to hyperlinks. (They are <u>underlined</u>.) When you click on a link with a <u>julie@shesite.com</u> format, your main email program (Outlook as an example) will automatically open up.

The email address in the link will appear in the "Send to:" field of your email program. Note: You don't have to be connected with the internet to write the email, but you have to connect before you send it.

Emphasis: There are a few really important ideas I don't want you to miss. So to make it easy and clear, you'll see various techniques throughout the guide to make words and phrases stand out. Certain words and phrases will pop out in bold text. A few words that I want to express a stronger tone or add vocal emphasis are written in *italics*. When you see phrases that are **bold and highlighted**, I hope you sit up and pay special attention to them.

Exercises: Any time you see **Exercise** that means get your journal. Grab a pen or pencil and write down your thoughts. The benefits in your life will increase exponentially when you actually do the exercises and journal your thoughts and feelings.

Tell Your Own Story

This is where you get to be a famous screenplay writer. Share your story, play your part, and express yourself fully on the pages of your personal journal. I encourage you get a special notebook or journal just to record your revelations from this amazing journey.

- Find, buy, make, or get a hold of blank reams of paper.
- Go into the archives of old empty notebooks, spiral bound, legal pads, or journals you bought but never used.
- Print these pages and staple them together.
- Take a special shopping trip to buy a beautiful new book – one that will hold your most intimate thoughts and revelations.
- Pick up a pen that feels fabulous in your fingertips – or select a variety of colored markers, crayons, pencils… whatever you fancy.

You will want to record all of your ideas and creative inspirations, especially when you see Exercise.

Decide on one fabulous spot that will hold and cherish all your exercises and innermost thoughts. Every page of this guide will present you with a new question, idea, or opportunity to reveal your core happiness so you can live vibrantly.

Discover new revelations and let fresh perspectives float through your heart, mind, and spirit. Some you may keep going back to, over and over. A few you will record just for clarity. And others you may forget about instantly, but they will still profoundly affect your life and subconscious mind. Tracking your revelations and breakthroughs is a marvelous way to add happiness to your life years from now. You'll have proof of how far you've come!

Use your journal to record your joyful process and progress. Write down anything and everything that comes in to your mind – no matter how simple, silly, scary, fun, or deep – each idea will open your heart and awaken your truth. Embrace this journey and prepare to travel "journal by your side" – wherever you go. You'll feel marvelous the first time you have a spontaneous inspiration in the middle of your work day and your journal is sitting next to you. Let your writings and discoveries take you away. Reveal lots of joy anywhere – anytime.

Wishes Do Come True

My wish for myself is that you stay intimately connected on this playful journey: To yourself, your journal, the people you love, and me, too! It's amazing when you think about it, how many of us share the same path. I am thrilled and delighted to share in your revelations and breakthroughs. We are more similar than we are different. Your insights can and will unleash a whole series of new discoveries in me – and in women around the world. I hope you will share all of your joys, frustrations, ideas, breakthroughs, and any questions that come to mind. Email: julie@shesite.com.

My wish for you is that you listen with your heart – more than you think with your head. Think With Your Heart Instead Of Your Head Do what feels marvelous and wonderful to you! Find a place in your body that you can connect with and know – beyond a shadow of a doubt – that you are exactly where you should be. Forget about what I (or anyone else) had in mind for you.

Wonderful woman (p.s. that's you!)… you and you alone are the expert of your life and destiny. Stay deeply in touch with yourself, trust your gut, and let a sea of new revelations, solutions, and life inspirations wash over you. I am certain all of the answers are inside of you. *Shout From The Rooftops In Your Stilettos* will pave the way for your inner knowing to direct you. Toss out any expectations right now and delight in the joy of the journey.

My wish for the world is unstoppable confidence that covers the planet! My dream is to see every woman who was once consumed with nervous, negative, or insecure energy shouting praises of self-confidence... roaring in laughter... celebrating deep self-knowledge. I wish for ultimate freedom and unlimited self-expression for every woman... which (I believe) leads you straight to more happiness and life fulfillment.

I hope *Shout From The Rooftops In Your Stilettos* inspires women everywhere and that someday I get to meet tons of silly, fun, frolicy, and supremely confident girls on the street. I hope to see the inspired look in their eyes – a look of certainty, hope, faith, love, and trust. Fears that once gripped them have almost all washed away. They stand tall, valiantly on a steeply pitched roof with arms wide open radiating unstoppable energy. They wear a warm, contagious smile where confusion once lived... AND it doesn't stop at those rosy cheeks but goes all the way to the core. And then sometimes (if I have my glasses on) I can look up and see a host of women high above the cityscape full of love and vitality with their skirts flippin' up in the wind like they just don't care!

> *"Three grand essentials to happiness in this life are something to do, something to love, and something to hope for."*
>
> Joseph Addison

Blaze Your Own Happy Trail

Just by purchasing this guide, you've already made an inner commitment to seek happiness and love in your life – and live in harmony with your values.

During our time together, you will begin to feel far more satisfaction, love, peace, happy passion, connection, gratitude, creativity, wisdom, and abundance! If you don't... you just call, write, scream, or shout over my way and tell me what's up immediately and without delay: julie@shesite.com. I wouldn't say it if I didn't mean it. Really. Try me.

Even though my tone is typically light and free flowing... and because for most of the guide we'll loosen up, lighten up, let go, and break a whole bunch of those society-imposed rules ... it's really important that I ask you – right now – to take just a moment of sincere seriousness. With stillness and admiration... I honor you.

Visit www.shesite.com. Streaming genuine happiness in your life today... and everyday!

7

I honor you for taking a risk and trusting yourself, for trusting me and opening yourself up to the process. I invite you to set your intention and commitment so you stay truly connected to yourself and reveal happiness that fits for you. Use *Shout From The Rooftop In Your Stilettos* to think about, journal, and emotionally connect to each and every exercise... so more happiness soaks in to your life.

Stop for a moment.

Settle your mind and body.

Breathe deeply.

Let go of the tension in your shoulders and your face.

Take one small step to pick out which stilettos you want to balance on. What color are they? How do they look on your perfectly manicured toes? How do you feel in them? How will you feel when you are shouting your praises from the rooftops in them? (hint... hint... you can even write this visualization in your journal if you want!)

Exercise

- Write in your first and last name.
- Make a personal commitment to yourself.
- Read it out loud.
- Date and sign it.
- Tell someone about it (if you're feelin' sassy).

I, _____ , agree with loving and thoughtful attention and intention that I will joyfully dedicate a small amount of time everyday to connect with myself and the ideas in *Shout From The Rooftops In Your Stilettos*. I promise to soak in these inspirational messages, carry out the exercises, embrace and customize simple healing strategies, play with simple meditations and rituals, engage in rich dialog, journal my feelings, and write from my heart.

I will be honest with myself and joyfully seek out happiness that fits for me. I expect nothing less than happiness, self-love, and appreciation to reveal itself to me throughout this magnificent journey. I will reflect on the exercises and take small actions to reach far beyond, stretch to greater lengths, and achieve lasting happiness that's just right for me, my work, and my life!

Date:

Signature:

Whoo-hoo!! You're awesome – blossom!

I'm so excited to see you make a commitment to your own happiness. Many other women will never take this bold step. I applaud you.

Ready to blaze it? I can almost feel your excitement. Your brilliant life awaits you. Let's jump up, dive in, and shift things just a bit so you can begin to truly love yourself, see your truth, and appreciate the life you live. Marvelous!

Feeling Nervous? *That's normal and natural. Instead of diving right in feel free to start with <u>A Little Fear In Passion</u> and continue through the From Fear To Passionate Flight chapter. Remember, I'm right here to hold your hand… it was scary for me, too.*

Oooooh… ooooh… I'm bouncing for you!

Let's ditch the seriousness and let the play begin! I hope your journey is filled with more love, peace, joy… success, abundance, prosperity… health, productivity, and blissful happiness.

"Action may not always bring happiness; but there is no happiness without action."

Benjamin Disraeli

Happiness Is A Moral Obligation

How much happiness do you desire? Take a moment to think about it. Or better yet, pull out your fabulous and fancy journal.

Exercise

- How important is happiness in your life?

Pretty pause. Think deeply about this question. Is happiness something that would be nice to have and wonderful to feel? Do you think you'd be fortunate if more happiness just happened to surround your life? Or do you think happiness is as essential to life as I do?

Is it crucial, fundamental, and primary to your existence? You may not have heard it put quite this way before, but I agree with Dennis Prager who says, **"Happiness is a moral obligation."**

It's normal to think happiness is a selfish desire, but I believe your happiness is just as important for the people you work, live, and come into contact with! Have you ever been around someone who is a total "Debbie Downer?" Ridiculously negative? Unbearably miserable? Everyone they come into contact with is oozed with a 'Ghostbusters-like' slime of pessimism? They have choices – but they sure don't pick happiness. Instead, they make a decision to focus on the negative. You have a choice as well.

Daily, you can decide how you choose to show up in the world. You can influence the world and the people around you in a positive and productive way, or you can sulk, complain, and make everyone else miserable, too.

Contrary to popular belief; **happiness isn't by happenstance. It is a byproduct of your intention and effort.** The happier you intend to be… the more you work on it and desire it… the happier you will feel. Decide on how happy you want to be.

"Happiness is not a matter of events;
it depends upon the tides of the mind."

Alice Meynell

Happiness Is More Than A Feeling

How happy do you want to "be?"

Happiness is much, much more than a feeling. Negative conditions, situations, and experiences are going to spring up around you everywhere. You won't always feel happy.

In fact, I'm certain you don't expect *Shout From The Rooftops In Your Stilettos* to cure all your unhappies. Do you? Well, we both know that would be crazy talk! Plus, you haven't seen me in one of my fits of fury. Oh yea, I could pass along some solid references if you ever wanted to inquire how mad, angry, pissed off, and red-faced I've become in the past. And even though (in the moment) I am livid and beside myself, it doesn't change who I am at my core. I am still an incredibly loving (and happy) woman – expressing an instant of fierce anger!

You will continue to get hurt, feel sad, be disappointed, and become angry. Life has a way of continually showing a spectrum of emotions. The beauty is this: **just because bad things are going on around you** (maybe you aren't beaming a smile as bright as the midnight stars) **it doesn't mean you are an "unhappy" person.**

When bad things happen (either now or in the past) and you aren't feeling like a bowl full of cherries or like making the proverbial lemonade – it ain't no thing. You are entitled to each and every feeling: sadness, depression, hurt, anger, disappointment, frustration. It does not change the woman you are at your core.

Exercise

Who are you when you are at your best?

- What would you like to experience more of?
- Return to a time when you could freely play in the sunshine as a child, how did you feel?
- What do you deeply desire for yourself?
- What do you wish for and want to feel more of?

Allow yourself to see all that is possible for your life. Look at some beautiful moments of glory in your past, allow yourself to imagine, visualize, and tap into more of them each and every day.

As you begin to look inside of yourself and get in touch with your feelings and emotions, your truth will rise to the surface. Begin to discern your own truth. Play an extreme sport with me: **extreme self-knowledge**.

As you reveal the authentic you, you will feel all the experiences life dishes out – but not become them. Knowing the difference allows you to be a whole and happy human even when bad things happen. You will return to your core.

*"It is not easy to find happiness in ourselves,
and it is not possible to find it elsewhere."*

Agnes Repplier

6.5 Billion Ways to Happiness

There is certainly no shortage of ways for you to live a happy and vivacious life – Dennis Prager estimates 6.5 billion in his calculated approximation (or the number of people in the world). Of course, *Shout From The Rooftops In Your Stilettos* doesn't cover all them… phew for your little eyeballs and busy fingertips! We could grow quite old here together.

On second thought… that doesn't sound bad to me! <u>The Rocking Chair Test</u>

The thing about this journey is that it is 100% personal and unique… just like your happiness.

You'll soak in a few ideas that seem to fit just right for you; others you will have to modify. Some will be so far off you'll roll your eyes and think I've lost it. But my hope is this: in the end you'll throw on your stilettos, strut your stuff, and live your life in the way that is perfectly suited just for you. Perhaps like the comfiest pair of jeans put on the planet – just for you and your fabulous body.

No matter what I say or what anyone else is doing, remember there are an infinite number of ways to live a happy and full life. Let's discover a few new ways on this journey and revive some of your old favorites that you forgot all about. If you're feelin' extra sassy, grab your journal and reveal a few personal pleasures.

Exercise

- Start to make as long a list as you can of things you enjoy.
- Pick a date and schedule one of these pleasurable activities right into your calendar.
- Make yourself a note and put it somewhere you will see throughout the day.
- Honor this activity with the same priority and commitment you would any important appointment.

pssssst... by the way...

did I remember to give you unadulterated permission to think about you and you alone?! If I didn't yet, I encourage and invite you to be incredibly opinionated and resolute about what feels wonderful and to truly go for what you want! Just thought now was a good time to mention that.

*"Remember that happiness is a way of travel,
not a destination."*

Roy Goodman

IT'S ALL ABOUT YOU

I Go Here

We all have basic human needs. Maslow mapped out a basic plan. First... water, food, and zzz's. Followed by safety, security, and stability. Beyond that we all want to be loved, appreciated, and feel a **sense of belonging**.

I'm sure Maslow is brilliant, but I prefer the words quoted from Elle Woods in Legally Blonde, **"I Go Here!"** That's my silly way of saying, "I belong."

When you 'go here,' a sense of belonging, security, and safety is welcome to wash over you. You are able to confidently face difficult situations, challenges, and risky propositions. You overcome obstacles that would have otherwise held you back. When you 'go here' your human need for belonging is satiated.

On the other hand, I'm sure you have experienced times when you didn't 'go here.' At a social event, for example, you didn't know a single person. You might have felt shy, awkward, and uncomfortable, or even experienced some physical pain. Any way you slice it, when you aren't feeling like your sassy self, you 'miss the party.' You aren't showing up as the vibrant woman you typically are... and have the potential to be. Your stilettos are stuffed in the far corner of your closet and your true, authentic self hides beneath a different and fearful girl.

Now, think about a day that you were on... rock-star on! Remember a time that you took the spotlight and shined (maybe without even realizing it). You walked gracefully in your stilettos. You felt confident and proud! Looking around you, you saw that the most loving, honest, and supportive people were right there by your side. You felt like you could take on anyone and anything!

Belonging is the fuel, foundation, and courage that will propel and drive you to go after your dreams. It lets you live with more verve and less fear. You won't be consumed with that nasty hesitating "fear of failure" or the fear of falling down and going... BOOM! You can take long strides in your stilettos.

Balanced. Confident. Courageous!

Cultivate a deep sense of belonging within your own heart and allow it to grow stronger and stronger as you reveal all the wonderful parts of you.

Exercise

Feel a sense of **"I go here"**

- Close your eyes and feel the pulse of your heart.
- Feel the nourishment your heart gives to your entire body.
- Be present in the moment and feel the love and compassion in your heart connecting to all good things in the universe. You are part of a loving master plan.
- Allow yourself to focus in on one specific experience familiar to you: another person, a living animal, the flowers dancing in your garden, the flame of a candle.
- Write down this person, place, or thing that feels close to your heart now.
- Let the goodness of this relationship flow into your heart. Feel gratitude and joy.
- Feel the power of this love.
- Write down the feelings (and gifts) you experience from this relationship.
- Share these gifts and reach out to someone you love.
- Let this love grow and grow beyond what your mind may understand.
- Feel connected to other humans who deeply experience this same love, gratitude, and sense of belonging.

Use this simple meditation to connect on a regular basis with the people, places, and beautiful things that support your sense of belonging. Take mini vacations in your heart and mind. Travel to many places and seek relationships where you can 'go here.'

> *"Your chances of success in any undertaking can always be measured by your belief in yourself."*

Robert Collier

Flaunt The Fabulous You!

Warning: The following exercise might feel awkward or difficult. Society typically doesn't believe it is acceptable for you to talk about how great, wonderful, beautiful, and fabulous you are. You might hear mutterings of voices or old stories in your head saying, "Don't be self-centered. Be modest. What an ego! How narcissistic." I say, **"Girl, you don't say nearly enough fabulous things about yourself!"**

Bust out! Be bold! Think big! Start shopping for the sassiest pair of shoes. Pick up a pen, grab your journal, and find a sunny tiled roof. You have complete and total permission to flaunt the fabulous you!

Here are a few ideas to stir up your spunkiest self before you get started.

- No thinking. Just pure free-flowing energy in writing.
- No filtering. Let it come from within.
- Don't let your brain sneak in. Let it flow straight from your heart. <u>Think With Your Heart Instead Of Your Head</u>
- Pretend you are the ultimate observer standing outside yourself and looking in.
- Imagine you are writing a love note to someone you adore – someone who is very similar to you.

Exercise

- As quickly as you can, write down five things you admire, adore, and appreciate about yourself - we'll call these things strengths.
- How did you feel when you wrote them?
- Why do you think you felt that way?

We have been culturally conditioned to avoid exposing our greatness. Most women, even when they are given complete and total permission to write their little hearts out, still find tooting their own horn a very difficult thing to do. The good news is… we've got plenty of time and lots of play ways to do it!

Exercise

Tell your journal your secrets.

- Were you as honest as you could be about your strengths?
- What were the first five attributes that came to mind? Write those down if they were different.
- Did you hold back? Why?
- What strengths would you have written down if you knew there was absolutely no chance anyone else would ever see them?

Exercising the muscle of self-love is one of the most difficult tasks you will ever face. It's normal to shut down, close up, and feel fearful. Or in the best case scenario, you shout from the rooftops but with incredible modesty.

Why is it so easy to rant and rave, praise and applaud others but when it comes to little ol' you... you feel shy, awkward, modest and oh-so quiet?

> *"Once we believe in ourselves,*
> *we can risk curiosity,*
> *wonder, spontaneous delight,*
> *or any experience that reveals the human spirit."*
>
> E. E. Cummings

A Little Splash Of Crazy

You see it all! No one knows you better than you do. You know every thought, conflict, problem, concern, flaw, or perceived shortcoming that exists inside of you. You've got a microscope of a brain that blows up the little things to exaggerated proportions.

I remember looking into the mirror one day, looking deeply into my own eyes attempting to see what was inside of me. Do you want to guess what I saw?

I saw the dark parts of me. I saw all the thoughts that have passed through my mind even the ones I wasn't proud of. There were lingering negative emotions. Judgments about myself and others. Bad habits. The commitments I made to myself but never kept. In that very moment, I didn't see anything wonderful or fabulous inside of me. But, I did find some beauty in all that darkness.

Part of the reason I think humans are so darn unique and cool is because of the 'little splash of crazy' in all of us. We've all got it. **It's our quirkiness, goof ball ways, odd peculiarities, passions, obsessions, and even imperfections that make us colorful – and wonderful.**

Let me ask you, if you could choose to be 100% pure right now – assume you wouldn't need to learn another thing for the rest of your life – would you?

Think deeply about this question and journal your thoughts and feelings.

Exercise

- Would you choose all the depths of who you are? Or would you rather be 100% pure without any further change, growth, or lessons?

Surprisingly when I ask this question to women, almost every woman chooses to embrace her gifts, beauty, and flaws, too. I've only met one woman so far who said she would want to be 100%… and I think I saw her squirm a little when she went deep inside and looked at what her life would be like. I believe if you decide you'd rather be pure, it's just a matter of time before you will be bored out of your zonker!

What will you choose? Let me share a bit while you assess your position. As soon as you choose to accept your imperfections and 'splashes of crazy,' it becomes easy to reveal your innermost beauty. You won't have to stress-out, worry, or try to hide the real and authentic parts of you. They are you. Imperfections, impurities, and all!

You are an amazing woman, just as you are. Let me go on record as saying that my favorite people in the whole world all have huge 'splashes of crazy.' My list of crazy goes on and on… and it allows me to see some pretty cool and creative stuff within me.

Ready to crack open the door to your brilliance and reveal all your dazzling gems? Let's bring in the brilliant, beaming lights that shine through you.

"There are as many nights as days, and the one
is just as long as the other in the year's course.
Even a happy life cannot be without a measure of darkness
and the word 'happy' would lose its meaning
if it were not balanced by sadness."

Carl Jung

The Kaleidoscope Colors Of You

Let the wonderment of a kaleidoscope bubble up inside of you – just like when you were a giddy little girl. Remember the first time you saw a kaleidoscope? Even the most boring, simple, single dimensional thing became an explosion of color, patterns, and magic. Grab a kaleidoscope and let it help you begin your journey to expose your hidden beauty and talents.

The kaleidoscope is a simple little thing, isn't it? When you think about it it's all a matter of perspective.

Case Study: 7:00 a.m. Monday morning alarm sounds.

> Quickly I find myself in the routine of life. The moment I roll out of bed, I get sucked in. I hardly realize that I'm instantly caught up in the monotony of life. Long to-do lists, responsibilities, and obligations begin. It amazes me how quickly I forgot about all the simple things over the weekend that made me smile... the flowers that came home with me from the Farmer's Market, brisk walks, great music, the fresh smell of being clean after a hot shower, spontaneous snacks, a cold glass of water, impromptu get-togethers, long and inspiring chats, and a steamy cup of Earl Grey. How quickly I overlook the blessing of a brand new day!

Are you forgetting to become still and reflect on all the glorious things you do? Sit for a moment and allow yourself **to open up to how amazing you are... your gifts, contributions, talents, accomplishments ... all that you give and the immense value you create in the lives of people around you.**

Let's go deep! See more talents, personal quirks, flair, flash, and glitter welling up inside of you. There's gold there! And it's the secret ingredient to bringing you more happiness, success, balance, and abundance.

Jay Abraham's *Your Secret Wealth* program first opened my eyes to my secret talents bubbling below the surface. Now you can look inside at the vivid, vibrant, and beautiful parts of you, too. The ones that tend to get dimmed down or overlooked. Move deeper into your personal inventory. Get ready to:

- See yourself with 10 times more dimension, value, and abilities!
- See the possibilities in your life become clear and evident.
- Empower your life and view yourself from the inside out.
- Walk away with more confidence, skills, and personal advantages.
- Accomplish anything you desire without letting opportunities slip past you.

Exercise

- How differently would your life be if every morning you recognized your unlimited possibilities through the view of a child's kaleidoscope?

"It doesn't hurt to be optimistic. You can always cry later."

Lucimar Santos de Lima

Clearing Out The Clutter Of Your Mind

If you are like me you've got a gazillion synapses in your brain – firing all at the same time! Clearing out the clutter of your mind probably feels more like relocating your home and collection of "stuff" than doing a little sprucing up or spring cleaning.

I know it's easier said than done, but if you can lighten the load a bit... I'll bet you'll be able to see more brilliance shine through. Here's a quick five-step process to clear your mind and remove some of the road blocks that could keep you from seeing the magnificent parts of you.

1. Create Mind Space

Did you embrace your 'splash of crazy?' A Little Splash Of Crazy If you did, then you are a bit freer to let your hair down, release imperfections, and go to town! This new mind space allows you to eliminate some of the negative self-talk. See your 'splashes of crazy' as a unique part of who you are. Become more accepting of yourself. Replace self-judgment or blame with simple and enlightening observations.

2. Trust and Commitment

Trust yourself. Let go of any tension and completely commit to the task at hand. The next section requires your commitment – to truly go for it – to find the dazzling specks, flakes, and nuggets of gold within you. One of my favorite sayings by the wonderfully talented Jazz Gal, Karen Gallinger, is, "The gold lies behind the fool." When I finally trust myself and get rid of the self-expectation to perform, look, or act a certain way; I am astonished at the gifts that flow out of me. Let go and take small risks that put you smack dab in the middle of the game of life.

3. Focus and Attention

Stay in the present moment. Don't let your mind drift, get preoccupied, think ahead to the future or behind about the past. Be here right now! You'll have more fun in life when you live it for the moment without dwelling over mistakes of the past or using valuable energy anticipating the future. The present moment is the life you live…and truly all you are guaranteed to have.

4. Be Spontaneous

Let your natural self react and respond. The O.C. Crazies, a sketch and improv comedy group based in Santa Ana, California, were master teachers of this simple philosophy. The truth is, when you are spontaneous your mind doesn't have to think or second-guess your decisions. Your first reaction is usually the right one – natural, quick, confident, and authentically you. Let your spontaneity and energy dance inside of you and release the wonderment of you.

5. Look For Your Loveliness

Start a personal resource inventory. Get out your journal and with a clear mind begin to see your gifts. Take inventory of the loveliness of you. Develop great respect, appreciation, and knowledge for all aspects of your being – your life, your relationships, your gifts, opportunities, talents, skills, and the choices you make.

> *"If we could see the miracle of a single flower clearly,*
> *our whole life would change."*

Buddha

Quick Tips And Inventory Guidelines

Let's prepare for your in-depth personal resource inventory. Are you as excited as I am? I have a little insider information about how amazing this will be for you.

Quick Tips

- Trust the process.
- Go with the flow.
- Find a quiet space.

My only caveat to you is to remember that this process of self-discovery won't be complete in one sitting. It would be impossible. But if you have 30 or so minutes to set aside, you'll come up with an extensive list of goodies that will transform how you feel about yourself.

Guidelines

- Start general and move to more specific.
- Don't worry about any repeats.
- No editing for now. Let it flow and you can edit later.
- Write your little heart out. Let one idea flow immediately to the next. Let each gift remind you of yet another… and another.
- Think of it as an emergency response situation to bring out the absolute best in you. Your mind, body, heart, and soul react automatically.

Taking Inventory Of Your Brilliant Gifts

Grab your journal. You will be making a total of five different lists. Consider the quick tips and guidelines above, but remember there are no rules!

Exercise

1. Skills List

Start scribbling anything and everything you think you do well. What skills do you have? Maybe you took accordion lessons as a kid. Can you change your car's oil yourself? Do you have a secret recipe everyone raves about? List everything you do that produces an outcome or a positive result.

Maybe you are…

- a wonderful communicator and people feel energized when they are around you.
- an excellent writer and still send personal thank-you letters (very rare these days).
- an optimist and see the good in situations.
- a research queen and everyone comes to you for the most reliable and up-to-date information.
- the concierge of your family and friends, always recommending movies, restaurants, or shopping destinations.
- a wonderful cook, a health nut, or a food connoisseur.
- always helping people.
- creative or good with your hands.
- an extrovert and have a warm approach to meeting or connecting people.
- a player always seeking out spontaneous adventures or creating something magical out of something ordinary.
- good at managing people, places, or things.
- effectively working from home.
- running your household successfully, with lightning efficiency.
- a planner and organizer.
- someone who always makes people laugh.

- a real live GPS system – you have a innate sense of direction – and can find your way out of a labyrinth – no problem.
- the family peace maker.
- the woman who has a point of view that is unique and valuable.
- brilliant business negotiator.
- the life of the party.
- a confidant to many.
- an avid reader.
- a computer whiz and can understand and access information quickly and easily.

Start letting your mind play with all the small and sizable skills you possess. Maybe you are incredible at:

- inspiring people.
- listening.
- coaching.
- decision making.
- nurturing.
- understanding.
- uplifting.
- encouraging.
- team building.
- logic.
- creating things.
- reasoning.
- problem solving.
- intuitive knowing.
- candid communication.

Don't dismiss or discount anything. If it comes to mind write it down – all those things you simply take for granted and feel second nature to you... these are your gifts. I promise – not everyone has your talents and skills.

- Ask yourself, "What do people come to me for?"
- What do you do over the course of a day?
- What do people notice about you and comment on regularly?

2. Knowledge List

Write down any specialized knowledge or education you have. What are you familiar with? Even if it was years ago, what have you learned in your lifetime?

Start scribbling anything and everything you think you do well. You might be a hula-hoop champ – write it down! List everything you know something about.

What are you familiar with? What is your education? What specialized knowledge do you have? Even if you don't use it anymore... what did you learn in school?

- literature.
- arts.
- music.
- history.
- anything mechanical.
- artistic medium.
- magic tricks.
- anatomy and the human body.
- human nature (how people act or respond).
- travel.
- trivia.
- cultural beliefs or customs.
- sales.
- modern languages.
- communication techniques.
- sports.
- computer or information technology.
- systems or procedures.
- grammar.
- economics.
- geography.
- politics.
- event planning.
- interior or fashion design.
- plants, birds, or trees.

- food preparation.
- science.
- marketing or sales.
- accounting.
- specialty tricks (I cure hiccups).
- time saving techniques.

What are all the things you've learned in your lifetime? What information is coming up for you?

3. Relationships

This is a fun one! People make the world go 'round and I'll bet you know some amazing people. Look at how many people resources there are in your life and the connections you share. Who do you know?

Write down specific names of people you know. You might want to break relationships down into several separate sections. Begin with personal relationships...

- family.
- friends.
- relatives (distant relatives).
- social circle.
- neighbors.
- friends of friends.
- acquaintances.
- mentors.
- parents of kids' friends.

Consider all your work relationships. Include past jobs and think back as far as you can. Who do you work with now? Who have you worked with in the past? Who works...

- for you?
- under you?
- over you?
- beside you?

Who...

- hired you?
- trained you?
- trained with you?
- recruited you?
- replaced you?
- refers business to you?

Look at who you know in your daily activities. Who remembers you? Where do you...

- shop?
- dine?
- exercise?
- pick up your prescriptions?
- take your dry cleaning?
- get your car washed?
- go for a cup of coffee?
- park your car?

List people you may have hired...

- at home.
- personally.
- professionally.
- as vendors.
- as advisors.
- as contractors.
- to conduct professional seminars.

Add any person that comes to mind. When your fingers start to get woozy, take a little break and think about how you relate to each person. Is there a skill or knowledge resource that you forgot about? What skills are you reminded of that you can add to this list?

25

4. Silly Stuff

These are my favorite personal resources of all! They are authentically you and totally passion packed!

- How do you see yourself when you are at your best?
- How do your closest friends and family view you?
- What about your colleagues?
- What are your quirks?
- What would you do all day if you could get away with it?
- What do you love talking to people about?
- What never bores you?
- What makes you feel alive?
- What's unique about you?

The Unique Game Imagine we are at a party and we each have to write down three totally unique things about ourselves. You want to be as unique as possible because if anyone else has the same thing, you have to start over from the beginning and come up with three more. Keep playing the "Unique Game."

- *Instead of saying that I traveled to the Czech Republic try, "I was standing in a Laundromat in Prague on September 11th when I first saw the twin towers fall."*
- *Instead of saying, "I love Whose Line Is It Anyway," try "Sometimes I call Wayne Brady my 'boyfriend.'"*
- *Instead of saying, "I love eating salads," try, "I cut my salad up into insanely small bite-size pieces and sometimes take more than 15 minutes before I will take my first bite."*

Call me 'crazy,' but I could play all day long. Let all the silly and fun stuff slide out on the pages here. Keep writing no matter how silly, crazy, or nonsensical it seems, put it down. Send your top three "totally unique things" to: julie@shesite.com.

Then run these silly skills through the skills, knowledge, and relationship lists. My Prague example reminded me of one person I met in Prague and still keep in touch with periodically in Los Angeles. I'm also reminded that I once spoke conversational Spanish, but would never have put it on my list because I can barely understand a word today. Let your list grow long and lovely.

5. Physical Resources

Finally! What most people would think of as your most important resources – your physical assets. But I say these resources don't hold a candle to the brilliance inside of you. Money, savings, and paid-off mortgages can't compete with the beauty of what is in your heart, mind, and spirit. Still… worldly possessions are important and valuable. List them all here:

- home.
- savings.
- financial resources.
- investments.
- automobile.
- art.
- valuables.
- collectibles.
- equipment.
- supplies.
- rental property.
- toys.

Consider the power of ingenuity, resourcefulness, and intangibles:

- access to information or certain types of things.
- techniques and processes you do really well.
- extra space.
- guest rooms.
- residual benefits of something you did in the past.
- information or projects you worked on but didn't do anything with.
- intellectual property.
- underutilized personal assets.

Even if something doesn't strike you as a huge financial asset, list all items that are important, meaningful, and valuable to you. Consider what you could trade or barter. Do some of your other skills come up – ones you hadn't thought of before?

Celebrate!

Wow!... let all this sink in for a moment. You arrived with an open mind and like a famous artist you took a blank tablet of paper and **remade yourself into a goddess of gifts**.

You are the artist of your life... your essence, your core, is where all this came from. No one's sheet will ever look the same. You are creating and embracing all the fabulous parts of you!

Use this palate of colorful gifts to create, recreate, or enhance yourself. And keep adding wonderful skills as they come to mind. If you're not sure where it fits, put it in the silly section.

> *"The more you praise and celebrate your life,*
> *the more there is in life to celebrate."*
>
> Oprah Winfrey

YOU'VE GOT CHOICES

Pick A Pocket Full Of Priorities

Even if you've heard the story before, open your heart and mind and pretend it's your first time. Let the *feeling* of Stephen Covey's big rock story soak into your heart, mind, and body. Imagine you are the elements and enjoy this famous visual that will prepare you for a strong and steady foundation atop your magical rooftop!

Stephen Covey placed a clear wide-mouth gallon jar on the table in front of him. Next to the jar was a collection of dark gray polished stones the size of your fist. He carefully filled the jar with the smooth stones, until he could fit no more.

"Is the jar full?"

He then pulled a large bowl of smaller polished stones from under the table. Gently pouring the pebbles into the jar, they nestled against the larger stones.

"Is the jar full?"

He reached for yet another bowl, this one filled with pure white sand. The sand flowed into the jar and hugged every last space not taken by the stones and pebbles.

"Is the jar full?"

Finally, he reached for a pitcher of sparkling water and poured it into the jar until it was filled to the very tip-top.

"What is the moral of the story?"

If you don't put the big stones in first, you'll never get them all in! **Get the important things in your life figured out first**. Then fit everything else around them. Make room in your life to celebrate what's truly important! If the big stones are your priorities, why in the heck are all the pesky pebbles and sandy bottoms buggin' you?

We hurry, scurry, and scamper so fast everyday that we forget to set our lives up to honor the most important priorities. Let's look at the very important things – priorities with a capital "P".

Exercise

No more sandy bottoms!

- How does it feel in your life when all those pesky pebbles, sand, and water surround you at every turn?

- Imagine you are a big stone at the bottom of the jar. What would you want to say? How would you feel if you were this rock?

- Would you feel the weight of the other elements pressing down on you? What physical sensations would you experience? Tension in your shoulders? A tight neck? A bit suffocated or fearful?

Start to become deeply in tune with how you feel physically and emotionally. When you feel any of these negative sensations in your heart, mind, or body… Stop! Take a moment and see if you are focusing on the big rocks. Chances are when you are focusing on your priorities, stress, worry and big burdens you carry will fall away. Let the rocks set your priorities and inspire your freedom!

> *"Happiness can be defined, in part at least,*
> *as the fruit of the desire and ability to sacrifice*
> *what we want now for what we want eventually."*

Stephen Covey

The Rocking Chair Test

Let's forge forward, look ahead and prepare for a brilliant life. "Start with the end in mind," as Stephen Covey would say.

Imagine you are 100 years old lounging in your rocking chair. As you think about your life in the context of this jar, what will you be thinking about and reflecting on? The rocks or the sand? What do you think you will fondly remember and smile back on? Chances are you will probably forget about the guy who cut you off on the highway or the rude server who practically ruined your dinner. (Starting to get a sneaking suspicion that these are some of my pet peeves?!)

I doubt you'll be dwelling on the lingering items you didn't cross off of your 'to do' list. You might, however, remember the boy at the grocery store who was once cooking Mother's Day dinner for his mom and asked you which onion to buy in the produce section. He was so grateful that he hugged you and wished you, "Happy Mother's Day!"

You'll remember the people, your friends, closest family members, and precious moments that nourished your soul. You'll remember the simple, happy, and profound peak life experiences you lived. <u>Peak Life Moments</u>

I am quite fond of this amazing and beautiful woman who recently celebrated her 91st birthday. She looks amazingly young for 90-plus years… and strong. She prides herself on still being able to beat some of the strongest 30-year-old men in arm wrestling contests.

As she gazes at herself in the mirror on the day of her birthday, she doesn't see the well-preserved, strong woman that most people see when they find out she's 91! She sees the extra wrinkles, the grey roots coming through, and her teeth in the glass on the counter.

But it's not the outer beauty that she is searching for… she peers into the mirror looking to see if her soul is sound. Just a little check in after 91 years of livin' to see if she really lived. Is she satisfied with her choices, her pursuits, and her dreams? Does she now exude the kind of inner happiness that comes from sincere, honest, and passionate living? The kind that comes when you take a hard look at what you want, accept it, and get up the nerve to face it head on? Is her life an example of dreams come true?

She whispers to herself in the mirror, "Jessie, you shouldn't have saved the expensive stuff for special occasions." … "You should've cleaned less and played more." … "You should've taken that painting and writing class." … "You should've worked with Walt Disney or tried to become a professional tennis player. Gosh was I good!"

And when you think about it… her life isn't over. She can march right out there to the dining room, dust off the good china, and hire someone to throw the most extravagant dinner party of her day and never lift a finger. She can cherish her long walks on the pier and feel blessed for her healthy body that carries her briskly to the end. She can take a painting or a writing class.

But the one thing she cannot change, no matter how strong and healthy she feels, is that too much time has passed to work with Walt Disney or play professional tennis. And this is terribly hard for me to admit, but sometimes it is simply too late. She waited too long.

Yes, I believe with all of my heart that the universe hears our deepest desires and wishes. I believe everything we desire is possible. So, it really breaks my heart to know my 91-year-old grandma has regrets and reflects on things she should've done.

How much longer will you continue to say, "I can't do it now?" ... "I'll do it later." ... "I need to save up some money." ... "The timing isn't right." ... excuse after excuse... you never seem to make time for the important things.

Stop making excuses! Commit to the big rocks. When you look at your life with the end in mind and start focusing on the big rocks, I suspect a sense of joy, happiness, and delight will wash over you. That's because you are paying attention to your personal priorities.

Exercise

- Are you doing what it takes to pass your rocking chair test?
- What can you do right now to enhance your rocking chair memories?
- Why not now? Today? This week? This minute?

> *"You don't get to choose how you're going to die, or when.*
> *You can decide how you're going to live now."*
>
> Joan Baez

You Are A Powerful Magnetic Attractor

What if your mind was only full of the brightest, most effervescent, sparkling, vivacious, and positive thoughts? As you continue to reflect back on the past, pick a time and day where you felt like your energy was off the charts! Have you ever had one of those amazing days? Where everything seemed to go just right? It just flowed... without you even trying!

Certainly you've had one in your lifetime.

Maybe the sun was shining. The air smelled clean and fresh. You got the parking spot right up front. You walked into a room and felt like a million bucks. Everyone around was great, helpful, happy, kind, and supportive. I believe there is a very good reason for this. You are a powerful, attractive magnetic force... and so is your mind.

Think of your mind as a huge magnet. The kind that attracts bright shiny objects from far away. A magnet doesn't try to attract, it just does. If you were a good lookin' paperclip and a magnet strolled by, next thing you'd know... you'd be stuck!

People have the same magnetic qualities. **We attract people, things, and opportunities whether we know it or not.** So why not use your wonderful God-given power to attract more of what you want in life?

The universal law of attraction makes one simple claim; you get what you focus on. And, like most laws of the universe, it is in effect 24–7, 365 days a year (366 on leap year)!

Your happiness starts with the thoughts you select. Pesky negative ones floating around in your gray matter not only make you feel lousy, but they invite their friends to come along. Next thing you know you have a whole gang of negativity.

Think back to a time that infuriated you. Did you replay the situation over and over in your mind? Did you reel back to other similar situations where you felt just as frustrated, mad, angry, resentful, or wronged? That's normal. It's the universal law of attraction in full swing.

Whatever it is you desire, think about it first in a positive way and you will begin to create your reality. If you want more love, give more love. If you want more happiness, feel more happiness. If you want respect, admiration, and appreciation, give it up… and give it first!

Exercise

Attract from the heart.

- Think about what is right and good in your life right now. What could you do to bring more of that into your life?
- Picture your heart as a powerful magnet. Allow and invite in more people who have the same values, beliefs, and positive perspective as you.
- When you find yourself in a difficult situation, change the dial of your mind. Pick a different station of thoughts to listen to and focus on. Find an inspiring channel that supports your desires and happiness.

Did you know that right now you can expect to see about 2% more happiness in your life? Just by learning that your thoughts attract things – and that those thoughts manifest in your life – you receive benefits.

*"Happiness is a perfume which you cannot pour
on someone without getting some on yourself."*

Ralph Waldo Emerson

33

The Positive Power Of Your Thoughts

Have you been thinking about what is really great in your life? Close your eyes and take a deep breath. Open them and ask yourself, "What is great about this very moment in time?"

If you truly reflected on what's right and then let yourself gallop through fields of possibility... I suspect you were able to see more and more goodness welling up. Sit with uncluttered thoughts about what is right in this very moment.

- Do you feel a little better?

- Feel yourself sitting a little taller?

- See the possibilities for your life?

Even if you felt better and saw the possibilities, eventually (and probably rather quickly) you may have slipped back into future to-dos and past what-ifs. All the "stuff" going on in your life started to come to the surface. You were reminded you haven't planned for dinner, returned week-old messages, or grabbed the mail. You went right back into your regular responsibilities almost instantly.

Where did that positive, bright, happy, inspired feeling go? **Your thoughts influence your emotions.** Once Gloomy Gus gets in, it's harder for the bubbly you to break through.

It is easy and natural for your mind to revert to what is wrong or linger in the negative. Here's the cool part – it only takes a bit of focus, attention, and intention to dismiss some of the pesky negative thoughts floating around your gray matter. Kick some lousy lingerers to the curb and make room for Positive Pollyanas! Make some of those negative thoughts pack up, move out, and find a new home.

Spend time reveling in wonderful moments of joy, contentment, inspiration, laughter, love, and learning... even when you don't necessarily feel like it will be directly proportional to your health, happiness, success, satisfaction, productivity, and fulfillment!

And on the days you think optimism is out, positive thinking is overrated, or a rosy attitude is completely out of fashion just remember this:

> *"The average pencil is seven inches long,*
> *with just a quarter-inch eraser."*

Robert Brault

Exercise

Put down your pen (or pencil) on this one and maintain a healthy outlook through the power of a positive thought!

- Think about doing something and spending time with someone you love deeply.
- Think about doing something wonderful for yourself that you would have never normally done.
- Think of someone new greeting you with a wonderful, bright, and radiant smile acknowledging, seeing, meeting, and accepting you for who you are.
- Think about how much life, beauty and possibility surrounds you today.
- Think about the note you received from someone for no other reason than to say how nice they think you are.

> *"If you realized how powerful your thoughts are,*
> *you would never think a negative thought."*

Peace Pilgrim

Act As If

I was so tired and worn out the other day. I walked into the kitchen and the only words I could muster up were, "I'm exhausted." Which now seems like a really big word for how tired I really felt, but it was the only response my lips would utter.

My boyfriend, David, said to me, "Wow Julie, I hear that you are really tired." Something in his voice and the way he said it jolted me. I instantly realized that in my pooped out pity party I was never going to feel better. So I picked up my shoulders and started walking around the house like a big dork saying...

"I am energetic."

"I feel good."

"I am happy."

I felt like such a phony. The words were coming out of my mouth, but I didn't believe them. And on top of that, I know all the theory. You'd somehow find out (cuz nothing I do seems to be a secret)... you'd call me out as total fake because I couldn't even listen to my own advice... and then I wouldn't have a shred of self-respect left and could never face you again.

So I carried on with my nonsensical talking. Trying to pick up my feet and toss my distrust and reluctance out the window. Eventually my feisty self took over and I started singing the sentences in a snappy tune. Louder and faster but still with this sassy tone you'd hear from kids just after they'd rolled their eyes.

"I am energetic."

"I am playful."

"I am happy."

I'm pretty easy to entertain and I knew I had nothing to lose so I kept at it. But I have to tell you, in that moment I truthfully didn't see how my chatter was going to give me more energy. But it did!

I started feeling better! I repeated the phrases and thought about times in my life, moments, and experiences that I felt really happy...

"I am silly."

"I am full of life!"

"I radiate light!!!"

"The strength of the universe supports me!"

My posture got better. I could almost feel the stilettos on my feet and the words that had no meaning whatsoever just three minutes ago started to sink in. Even writing them right now makes me feel lighter! I'm asking you... *pleeease*... even if you think I'm crazy and it won't work, try it once. For me? What do you have to lose?

I believe you can have anything you want and I believe you can change anything you desire. If it's health, money, happiness... success or peace of mind... act as if. Feel it in your bones. Speak it out loud and watch it manifest itself.

Exercise

- Make a list of how you feel when you are at your best. Or if you want to cheat you can use mine. But I bet you'll wanna make your own later.

- Sneak off somewhere and read them to yourself out loud. (Hint: The car is a great place if you're shy. You can even get some rhythm there and give them a beat too.)

- The next time someone asks you, "How are you?" instead of saying "Fine," "Ok," or "Good" ... say, "Wonderful," "Outstanding," or "Fantabulous!" even if you don't feel like it.

If you want to be a crazy, silly, break-out-of-the-box girl, try saying "Marvelous!" for a whole month. At first it will feel awkward and not real. But, if you stick with it, I promise that the days you start out feeling not so hot will be short ones because your sassy stiletto self will want to bust out, be positive, and really start to feel...

"Wonderful."

"Amazing."

"Stupendous" and "Spectacular!"

Did you know that you can expect extraordinary miracles to manifest about 25% more often when you learn that your thoughts become things, and then use positive and powerful visualizations several times a week to manifest what you want? <u>Become An Affirmation Aficionado</u>

"See the things you want as already yours.
Think of them as yours, as belonging to you,
as already in your possession."

Robert Collier

Irritations Inventory

Sometimes all this positive thinking stuff is much easier said than done. You've been there? The weight of the situation feels so big and heavy; it's really hard to get back and reconnected to the positive. I remember trying to shove out my negative thoughts one day. I'd been at it for hours before I called my cousin in despair pouting, "I know this stuff. What is my problem?!" Why is it so darn tough?

There are pesky things that get in the way of your positive energy. I fondly refer to it now as the "Suntan Pantyhose Syndrome."

One of my old desks at work had a pesky sliver of wood underneath that would run my pantyhose – almost every single day. What started as a small hole quickly turned into a fast moving run. For the rest of the day I'd poke at it, try to cover it up, complain about it and watch it travel like a very determined and fast moving marathon runner.

To this day it shocks me how long I let pattern go on. After buying and ruining dozens of packages of fancy hosiery, I finally took a little piece of scotch tape and stuck it under the desk to protect me from future snags.

Let me just say, that tiny piece of tape gave me so much peace of mind... I can't even begin to tell you! But how many days went by – fuming and fretting about the smallest, stupidest thing that I had complete control over?!

Exercise

- What bugs you?
- What's not right in your life?
- What are you not enjoying?
- What irritates the heck out of you?

Surface up the stuff you tolerate and look at every area in your life that you are not satisfied with. I mean everything...no matter how trivial it may seem. Just by writing down your irritations and taking an inventory on paper, many of them will transform or start to disappear. Seriously! It's trippy. Others will have simple solutions that seem to magically appear, like my scotch tape! Or just putting it all in perspective makes it seem less important.

It's amazing how free you will feel. These irritations and small burdens add up and create tension in your life that you don't even realize is there. Let's go stomp out those irritations.

Look at 'em. Release 'em. Get 'em all out. Irritations are just that… irritating! Get all worked up, if you must… just let 'em go and let 'em rip – the irritations, not the pantyhose

Exercise

Look at every area of your life and write as big an irritations list as you can. What's been buggin' you?

- Work.
- Home.
- Family.
- Career.
- Physical.
- Emotional.
- Money.
- Personal.
- Social life.
- Entertainment.

"Worry never robs tomorrow of its sorrow,
it only saps today of its joy."

Overcome Overwhelm

When you feel overwhelmed, remember you have choices. You can focus on what seems like the monstrosity of it all or you can take it one baby step at a time.

There are days that life throws bullet… after bullet… after bullet and I feel like Wonder Woman, deflecting almost anything. But when the Uzi of life starts firing, my super powers powder away. The rounds of responsibility are harder to deflect. And the absolute best (and only) way I know to skate through like a pro is firing back one bullet at a time.

Put it in perspective. Pick your battles. Let it go. Is it a big rock? Pick A Pocket Full Of Priorities Ditch the stress. Find the joy. Grab a friend and giggle. Look at the bright side and duke out all the remaining items with love and faith.

39

Exercise

Next time overwhelm starts to sneak in – because it's not a matter of if, but when – try the following exercise…

- Do a brain dump and get all the issues out on paper (or your journal).
- Ask yourself how important is this in the big scheme of life? Is it worth the stress?
- Think of the smallest possible action you can take to help you feel better and move forward.
- Trust the process.
- Think of what you can do to make it more fun and playful.
- Celebrate what you've already accomplished!
- Look at the worse case scenario. What is the worst that can happen?
- Let go. Remember how insignificant this will all seem a few weeks from now.
- Find the humor in it so you can laugh about it later – or now!

Get all the big and little stuff out. You will feel like a million bucks when your irritations have a place to live – a place that isn't in your mind. You've only got so much space in the mind queue. Kick out the Lingering Larrys that aren't all that important. If you don't, they'll just keep sticking around and buggin' you. Once you get them all out, we get to play in powerful action with a few of them and fill the space up with great stuff.

I do believe "active hope" is coming right around the corner… to the rescue!

"Nothing can stop a woman with
the right mental attitude from achieving her goal;
nothing on earth can help a woman
with the wrong mental attitude."

Thomas Jefferson

Active vs. Passive Hope

Passive hope happens when we tolerate stuff and hope it goes away, "I hope it will be better tomorrow." Ever felt you met your match with a rotten day and barely got through? You tolerated it. Thinking to yourself, "I really hope this gets better tomorrow." Monday's are super common 'hoping' days! Active hope is when you become proactive and do something to support a marvelous Monday!

Passive hope means you wish, think about, take a deep sigh, but never really do anything productive to change your circumstance or make it different. Active hope is where the rubber meets the road – where your stilettos meet the rooftop. In the simplest terms, active hope is still hoping, but hoping accompanied by action steps. Active hope is where all the hope inside stirs, stimulates, moves, and replaces stagnant wishing and wanting with life-changing growth and control. Your life becomes full of transformation and meaning.

Perhaps there are little tiny active actions you could take to add more joy to your Monday mornings. Instead of grumbling about another week ahead, make itty-bitty decisions that support you and your happiness today. Maybe it's:

- a sunrise yoga class.
- a coffee or your favorite beverage splurge on Monday mornings only.
- a weekly lunch date with someone you rarely get to see.
- when you wear crazy undergarments under conservative clothes.
- your scheduled time to dive into a good book, take a long bath, or watch a movie.

Exercise

- What are you going to do to wash away the Monday blues next week?
- What small decision will support you to start feeling happier today?
- Write three things that made you smile this week. What could you do to encourage more of that every day?

"The courage to imagine the otherwise
is our greatest resource,
adding color and suspense to all our life."

Daniel J(oseph) Boorstin

Irritation Recovery

When you embrace the idea of active hope, you hope for bright sunny days but come prepared with a toasty overcoat, umbrella, and a warm pair of boots in case the worst thunderstorm hits. It's doubtful that you would just walk out the house in summer attire if the weather man had predicted the worst storm of the season.

Pick up your irritations list, how do you feel? Have you been hoping for change to come out of nowhere? Or have you thought... and then taken small and simple actions that feel good and support you to make them go away?

Replace daily irritations on your list with an umbrella of active hope. Go back through your irritations inventory. Think about these three basic choices for each one.

- Let go of dull days and the daily irritations that go along with them. Can you truly let go? Forget? Forgive? It's my personal opinion that this choice is the hardest to embrace, honestly release, and officially let go of.
- Passively hope life and work get better.
- Or take specific, frequent, energetic, and simple actions that improve your situation and make the irritations slowly dissipate and finally fade away.

If you chose specific and simple actions, make your own Irritation Recovery list near the Irritations Inventory sheet.

Exercise

- What could you do to fix some of your irritations?
- Are there some solutions that come to you – some as simple as a piece of scotch tape?
- Go through each irritation and make three recommendations that will move you toward an active state of hope.

Hoping without action leaves you victim to external circumstances. With positive intention you can feel more control, peace of mind, and well being as you joyfully take a very small action to help you get the results you want!

"If you don't like something change it.
If you can't change it, change your attitude.
Don't complain."

Maya Angelou

Put It All In Perspective

Ever had one of those tiny things go wrong or back fire on you? A few seemingly small irritations build up and up and finally go... Ka- BOOM!

I remember getting a phone call from one of my closest friends a while back. Her normally cheery, loving voice was frantic and tense. She went straight into her list of woes and I remember not getting it. Seemed just like an ordinary day in her life. All the stuff she was listing off just didn't seem to equal the stress she was experiencing.

But to her, the last straw had landed flat on the proverbial camel's back!

She was overwhelmed and couldn't get her perspective back. Unfortunately (or maybe fortunately) she caught me right in the middle of my work day and in one of my abrupt, get-it-done-now moments. Playing in hard-core Monopoly-style solution mode: I passed GO. Did not collect $200. And went straight to work!

Ripping out a piece of paper, I asked her to recite back everything that was on her mind.

I scribbled and scratched.

- Potluck party.
- Lawn and leaves.
- Finalize kitchen remodeling.
- Daughter's piano lesson.
- A not-very-nice comment from her boss.
- She hadn't heard any news about a new project she was working on.
- Allergies and sneezing fits.

Got them all down and blurted out.

- Swing by the deli – 10 minutes to get a small party platter.
- Hire the 12 year old next door to mow the lawn and rake the leaves.
- Buy yourself another 7 days and tell the contractor for the kitchen to wait. It will be worth it.
- You have piano lessons every week!
- Your boss is a knucklehead, let it go – you know who is right.
- No news is good news!
- Allergies suck sweetie, no wonder you are feeling so crazy today!

We both rolled with laughter. It was just an ordinary day, but to her it felt so overwhelming. So often the plague of our stress can be remedied with a good friend, a new perspective, and a list.

"The greatest sweetener
of human life is friendship."

Joseph Addison

Forgive, Forget, And Make Amends

You are on a roll! Let's keep opening up more fabulous space for positive thoughts and really get to the bottom of some of those nasty lingerers. Look at some of the negative notions that might be loitering in your mind.

You probably already have a sense that there is no possible way you are going to clear up years of irritations or mind murkiness in a single day. But seriously, what is up with the greasy-spoon situations that stick around like a bad double-deck hamburger and chili cheese fries snack? You've been carrying them for far too long. Forgive, forget, and make amends. Your health and happiness depend on it.

I remember a run in I'd had with a close college friend. I had known her for almost 10 years. We were making plans to travel to South America together. She asked if I would be hurt if she didn't go and went with her new boyfriend instead. I replied, "Yes." I was honest, but supportive of her choices.

I found out a month later from a mutual friend that she was gone – traveling in Peru. She had gone without me… with him… the boyfriend. I was devastated. I quickly decided I didn't need friends like that and wrote her off. We didn't speak for months.

Almost 8 months later, she asked to see me. We met at an Italian restaurant and I came prepared to close the door to the friendship and never speak again. I felt like I had nothing to lose so I told her the facts and how sad, disappointed, angry, and embarrassed I felt. She listened.

I even went back years ago to a few small things we had never discussed. I closed the door to our friendship and told her I felt like our lives were moving in different directions.

I never would have expected her response. She explained what had been going on in her life at the time and much of it made sense. She felt horrible and apologized. She explained how she wished now she had called me before she left. She carried guilt and shame for months and wanted to reconnect and mend our friendship. A bit skeptical, I wasn't entirely sure I was ready to forgive her just yet.

We continued to talk and I began to see the beauty in her that I'd known for years. I saw some of the difficult times she had been going through and was able to see her as a caring woman who made a difficult choice. She was now facing her fear and asking for forgiveness. We rekindled our friendship and since wore our stilettos to her wedding celebration and the birth of her two sons. And, I even got to finally shout from Machu Picchu, too!

Exercise

Look deeply to see what unfinished business you need to tend to.

- Who do you need to sit down with and talk to?
- What do you still need to forgive yourself for?
- Who do you want to hear you?
- What expectations are you still hanging on to?
- What problems are you still trying to solve with force instead of forgiveness?
- What responsibilities have outlived their welcome?
- What self-judgments need to go?

These may have all been problems, behaviors, or opinions that served you once. Today, I say, you have a choice. You can keep them or create new beliefs, relationships, and attitudes about your life and personal circumstances. Be the bigger person. Make the call. After all, you are the one holding on to the grief and pain – not the other person. Allow yourself to forgive and make amends in the smallest way that feels good to you.

Don't You Wish *every person would do this exercise?! Imagine how wonderful the world would be! Send a quick note to a friend you know needs a gentle reminder.*

Exercise

- Write three little things that have been weighing on you heavily. Three things you know you need to forgive, forget, or change.

- Pick the easiest one and write another list of the tiniest actions you could take that would take less than two minutes.

- Break every item up into two-minute miracle actions so nothing stands in your way from feeling lighter and letting go.

This may be your start to moving the mountains (or mole hills) of pain, grief, stress, and fear. And remember… you don't have to do it all at once!

> *"Some tension is necessary for the soul to grow,*
> *and we can put that tension to good use.*
> *We can look for every opportunity to give*
> *and receive love, to appreciate nature,*
> *to heal our wounds and the wounds of others,*
> *to forgive, and to serve."*

Joan Borysenko

Dust Busting

I confess. I was a sweeper. You can see from my story above <u>Forgive, Forget And Make Amends</u> that when stuff in my world went wrong or felt frustrating I'd just look for a cheap way out. (or what I now refer to as my broom — so I could sweep the dust bunnies under the carpet) Sweep. Sweep. Sweep.

And I was good at it! Play nice. Dodge the difficult. Pretend nothing happened. Then try to deal with the spiraling stories, stress, and negative emotions that came from it. Slowly but surely I learned to face the scary stuff. What felt like pure torture at the beginning, became the greatest gift I could possibly imagine.

From the beginning my boyfriend, David, would poke and prod forcing me to communicate, share my feelings and express *only* the truth. I felt vulnerable, lame, and horrified at the same time.

But after a dozen or so times of this torture, a pattern started to emerge. Once the tough stuff was out and tears had been shed… we *always* became closer. I experienced moments of stillness and connectedness that is unexplainable. We bonded. Our relationship deepened. We started to reveal our true selves and grow from every experience. This happened time and time again until subconsciously I started developing a new set of beliefs –- unexpectedly.

I know it sounds corny, but over a very long period I started to view the negative experiences in my life as positives. I actually got excited when tempers would flair or misunderstandings ensue. The outcome was always positive and our relationship deepened.

Here's what is possible for you, too!

- Express your honest feelings without judgment.
- Get in touch with your true feelings knowing they are beautiful and healthy.
- Stop stuffing your feelings and release your self-inflicted condemnations.
- Clear the air so you don't have to pretend everything is "okay."
- Feel the peace of mind that results when your actions are in alignment with your true feelings.
- Gain respect of others instead of fearing you might lose their friendship.
- Communicate effectively without displaying passive-aggressive behaviors.

Exercise

- How different would your life be if you knew negatively charged situations would soon become wonderfully enlightening and positive?
- Visualize the positive benefits in your life when you successfully communicate through the most difficult conversations.
- Feel the benefits in your entire body.

It's easy to get caught up in the negative spiral. Day to day, look at how many people get caught up in it and end up carrying massive stress.

How would you feel if someone close to you got their feelings hurt from something you did? Or perhaps there was a misalignment or misunderstanding. Would you want them to come to you? Or hide their feelings and let the problem grow bigger – causing even more problems in the relationship?

I believe we are together now because you want to break through the difficult situations and give yourself more reasons to celebrate and feel happy in your saucy stilettos.

- The next time you face an incredibly difficult situation, playfully rejoice in your heart.
- See the problem and stare it down because you have enough love, strength, and courage inside of you to overcome it.
- Take a moment and try to come from a solution-oriented place. See it as an opportunity to learn something.
- Be loving and kind to yourself.
- Let go of your expectations or feelings that you have to say it just right.
- Speak from your heart and try to move away from feelings of defensiveness.
- Be true to yourself. Fully express yourself in the moment and let go of what could be ahead.

Celebrate! Pull up the carpets and let your wood floors shine as brilliantly as your heart. Clean up the dust bunnies with a joyful heart and a knowing of how marvelous you will feel when you've communicated your truth.

"It is very hard to say the exact truth,
even about your own immediate feelings — much harder than
to say something fine about them which is not the exact truth."

George Eliot

FILL UP WITH GOOD STUFF

Become An Affirmation Aficionado

Call them empowering thoughts, auto-suggestions, bridge beliefs, or just plain ol' affirmations, but just be sure you call them!

You cleared out some of the clutter of your mind so now you have space to fill up with good stuff. One of my top things to spread the word about is: affirmations. My fav! Listen closely for my squeals and Whooooo-hoos!

What's so mind-boggling is that I'm not sure I can even wholly explain why affirmations work, I just know they do! Call me an affirmation aficionado if you must, but I'm sold on the fact that **affirmations are the single most important key to a brilliant life.**

Anything is possible. You can do, have, and be anything you desire. When you use affirmations you make everything possible. It is because your subconscious mind takes all the orders and suggestions you give it at face value. It accepts every story, thought, and idea with the utmost faith and beauty. Pretty cool, huh?

The subconscious mind never doubts or questions you. It embraces the dominant thoughts in your mind as truth. The unfortunate part is that the average person fills their mind with far more negative messages than positive ones. Hence – my passion and plea.

EMBRACE AFFIRMATIONS!

You can use affirmations to retrain your subconscious mind. Use them to change anything you desire. Transform old patterns, embrace new thought processes, and watch effortless actions support the life you want to live.

Visit www.shesite.com. Streaming genuine happiness in your life today... and everyday!

49

An affirmation:

- Is a statement of positive fact.

Say it this way:	I have more money than I will ever need.
Not this way:	I am not broke.

- Is stated in the present tense.

Say it this way:	Top mentors love, trust, support, and guide me.
Not this way:	I will meet mentors to help me.

- Many times it begins with "I am."

Say:	I am silly, happy, full of energy, and a joy to be around.

- Can be said (or thought) anytime, anywhere.

Say:	I lounge outside on comfy and inviting patio furniture.

- Designed to create positive change in your life.

Say:	I am consistently organized and focused on my top priorities.

- Becomes more true and solid the more they are used.

Say:	I appreciate, adore, honor, and respect my lover.

- Is generally short and to the point (although this is a really hard one for me)!

Say it this way:	I wake up early - before 8:00 a.m.
Not this way:	I wake up early before 8:00 a.m. with a smile on my face to enjoy the morning and a triple shot latte in my professional stainless steel espresso maker with a fresh bran muffin.

Exercise

- Create a picture of your life by mind mapping every area of your life. See the <u>Irritations Inventory</u> exercise for sample areas of your life. Look at any areas you want to change.
- Write down one very specific thing you want to change in each area.
- Play a movie in your mind of what your life would be like if these things were certain and true.
- Create 3–5 affirmations that directly relate to the things above you most want to change.
- Say your affirmations out loud or focus on them silently in your mind while you play the movie in your mind.
- Repeat them daily.

Did you know that if you use the knowledge you have about the power of your thoughts... if you visualize and begin to say, do, and affirm the things you desire in your life, that the miracle of your success is practically unstoppable?!

> *"Our thoughts and imaginations*
> *are the only real limits to our possibilities."*

Orison S. Marden

Bridge Beliefs

You can have anything you desire in your life, but did ever think to yourself, "Na, that feels too big or grand?" I doubt I'm the only one.

Everyday, multiple times a day, I repeated the affirmation "I earn $91,578 a month." I would even write down a date, mark it on the calendar and visualize the money in my bank account. The dates would pass and nothing would happen.

Not only did I feel discouraged, but conflicting emotions coursed through my body. In my heart I believed the money, work, or jobs would appear. But my head doubted it was possible and stubborn weeds of doubt were planted in my mind.

Bridge Beliefs are exactly what you would suspect: **a belief that creates a bridge from your current reality to your ultimate desired future state.**

To Satisfy Your Curiosity
No, I have never earned $91,578 a month. Maybe someday I will; or maybe someday I won't. Either way, here's what's important: a phenomenal coach named Terri Levine (www.TerriLevine.com) allowed me to prosper through a different set of affirmations she calls "Bridge Beliefs."

Bridge Beliefs are:

- Something you truly believe in your heart.
- They don't force you to stretch your imagination.
- Better than old beliefs, but less than your ideal vision.
- Begin with really, really small baby steps.
- Eliminate conflicting emotions.
- Take you higher and higher, farther and farther without your mind telling you why it can't happen.

At times I still find it incredibly difficult to jump from where I am sitting today to my ultimate dream. Bridge beliefs have helped me breakthrough and overcome the chatter in my mind telling me why an affirmation won't come true. Dream as big and bold as you dare – then take one tiny step in your stilettos onto the bridge of new beliefs.

Exercise

- Look at your affirmations (either the ones you wrote in the last section or some that you currently use).
- Do they reflect a state of bliss?
- Are they so big and bold that you are almost shocked in disbelief?
- See if you can go back and make them even bigger, brighter, and bolder!
- If anything was possible… if there were no limits… and you were guaranteed to succeed… what would you dream up?

> *"People become really quite remarkable when they start thinking that they can do things.*
> *When they believe in themselves they have the first secret of success."*
>
> Norman Vincent Peale

Building Bridges To Where You Want To Go

Let's begin to bridge the gap between your present life and ideal future. It's easier than it might seem. We'll take it one small step at a time.

Exercise

Current Beliefs

- Draw 2 vertical lines to make 3 fairly wide columns in your journal.
- Title the first column on the far left "Current Belief."
- Title the middle column "Bridge Belief."
- Title the far right column "New Belief."
- Write at least five – but no more than 10 – "Current Beliefs" you want to change in your life. Tip: Look at your <u>Irritation Inventory</u> and rank your top irritations. Write what you currently believe about that situation in the first column.

Super! Your "Current Belief" column should be close to your reality. This is the space you live and exist in. Right?

Now, let's jump to the far right column "New Belief." Here's your chance to dream and aspire to a life and world that is utterly amazing! Look at the current belief and follow the instructions to write a "New Belief" on the same line in the far right column.

Exercise

New Beliefs

- Write your optimal state without flaw, want, or need – just as you would like to be living – in the "New Belief" column.
- Write each new belief in the present tense.
- Keep it short.
- Be specific.

Write it this way:	I am in love with the man (or woman) of my dreams.
Not this way:	I am in love.

True story. A friend of mine has been using affirmations to fall in love. She forgot to say 'with a man.' She did fall deeply in love – with a stunning stallion. She just bought a home and moved from the east coast to San Diego. United and in love with this magnificent horse, we giggle that she needs to be a little more specific next time. It is common to use affirmations and then get something you didn't exactly plan on.

- Think big. Does the new belief limit you in anyway?

Why limit the wealth and abundance the universe wants to give you in any area of your life?

Write it this way:	I will earn more than $91,578 a month.
Not this way:	I will earn $91,578 a month.

- Does the new belief make you smile?

Think big. Stretch far. Be brave. And go to town! Be sassy and paint your beliefs in full Technicolor using every color of the rainbow. Then use your upcoming bridge beliefs to center and ground the new beliefs… so they move you in your stilettos!

Ready to bridge? Get into the gap and bring it all together. Focus on the middle column of the page and begin to build your "Bridge Beliefs."

Exercise

Bridge Beliefs

- Write your bridge beliefs in pencil. (You'll see why in a moment.)

- Look at each belief in the first column "Current Belief." What is the tiniest affirmation you could speak that will start to move you toward the "New Belief." Write it in the center column.

- Dog-ear or bookmark this page in your journal. Review your bridge beliefs and amp them up once a week.

- When you feel yourself giggle inside and you think to yourself "Of course I believe that," you are ready to change the bridge belief.

- Keep your eye on your trajectory – "New Belief" – and write a tiny bit bigger "Bridge Belief" that keeps you moving.

- Celebrate your growth each time the eraser hits the journal and you amp up a bridge belief.

How will your life look a month, a year, five years from now when you have gone through dozens of erasers and you are living your life in full and fabulous Technicolor?

"Live your beliefs and you
can turn the world around."

Henry David Thoreau

Your Technicolor World

Feel the energy, vitality, and passion when you are living in this "New Belief" Technicolor world of yours! Really… *feeeeeeel-it.* The more feeling and emotion you add when you are speaking your bridge beliefs the more powerful they become.

It's a fact. **The brain does not differentiate fantasy from reality. The human brain responds the very same way when you imagine and feel an activity as if the situation was actually occurring.** This is a really juicy bit of info… what it means to you is that you can shift your entire life by thinking new thoughts. The thoughts create positive patterns and new beliefs. Your actions will begin to reflect these beliefs and manifest themselves in the form of success, achievement, and accomplishment! Add lots of feeling to your thoughts and affirmations to turbo boost your success.

Speak your new beliefs with feeling and emotion. Live them as if they are actually happening. Let your brain, body, and cells feel the experience. **When you mix the thoughts in your head with emotion, you create a magnetic force in your life where like attracts like.** Remember <u>The Positive Power Of Your Thoughts</u>? The strong attraction with feeling eventually shows up in a physical and very real way. Emotion makes the vision feel like it's really there. It becomes real and concrete.

A Little Caveat *The same principle holds true for negative thoughts. The ideas you focus on and put in the forefront of your mind will become your new reality. Thus, I could make an argument that worry is a prayer for something you don't want in your life.*

Exercise

- Include all five senses. Think about your beliefs as if they were a Technicolor movie. See and feel the vision of what you want – make it real, alive, breathing, and colorful.

- Don't worry about the "how-to" yet. Let that go for now. Just play. Dream. Visualize. Feel it in your heart. Let your thinking mind take a vacation.

- Create a long and lovely story or a fairy tale out of your affirmations and see yourself as a magnificent princess.

- Repeat your affirmations or bridge beliefs silently or out loud. Especially times you are in high emotional states. Play them like a movie. Repeat them at night and in the morning when your subconscious is most open.

- Learn expert affirmation hygiene. Make your affirmations and Technicolor visions a way of life – as regular as brushing your teeth every morning.

Examples of "high emotional states."

- Any time you hear fantastic news.
- You spontaneously feel a moment of joy and peace.
- Hear yourself laugh out loud.
- Hear your favorite song come on.
- Smell something you love.
- Hang up the phone after you've heard some good news.
- Feel alive and energized in the moment.

Exercise

- Create one all encompassing serenity slogan that accompanies you everywhere you go.

Repeat it morning, noon, and night with an intense feeling of celebration.

Samples:

- I love myself.
- I am good just as I am.
- My life thrives with goodness, now and forevermore.

> *"Your intellect may be confused,*
> *but your emotions will never lie to you."*

Roger Ebert

Think With Your Heart Instead Of Your Head

I've noticed the faucets of my creativity, joy, and flow slow down – or come to a screeching halt – every time my mind takes center stage on the big screen. At first I feel brilliant, creative, and witty. Playing in the movie of my life and enjoying the free flow of energy. But then I notice some scene changes up ahead. Instead of jumping into a new pair of stilettos and skipping ahead to play in the new adventure, my brain switches on to figure it all out and my ankles feel wobbly and unsteady.

But… wait! In the past it's been my natural skill, sense, energy, confidence, faith, and frolicy fun that steers me safely from one challenge, opportunity, and scene of life to another. A full pros and cons analysis of the new changes ahead are precisely what stop me in my tracks. I completely cut off the flow of energy. I start to wonder, over-think, and feel fear welling up. I see the potential risk and possible danger ahead.

The most powerful breakthroughs of my life didn't come from the 'heady' accounting "T" charts I made that listed my pros and cons. Too much brainpower without my heart involved clouds my clarity. The times I let go or called on my creativity, intuition, imagination, and silly solution finder, I saw new solutions and opportunities. Your playful, fun, and spontaneous self will literally bounce you in… out… and around every difficult situation if you are open to it.

If you had to choose between your heart and your head, which would you trust more?

You've got my permission to *feel* through some tough decisions you face. **When was the last time you made a wrong decision by listening to your heart or your gut?** How many times did you get that, "Geez, I knew it," feeling! You felt the signs early on. Your body gave you signals. If only you would have listened! But your head took over, rationalized, and analyzed the info and poof… your decision was final – only to later learn your gut was right on!

Free yourself from second guessing your decisions.

- Trust your instinct.
- Listen to your heart.
- Go with your gut feeling.
- Lean on your intuition for advice.
- Pay attention to all your senses.

*"Let your imagination release
your imprisoned possibilities."*

Robert H. Schuller

The Ba-Bum Of Your Heart

Don't take it from me; check out what science says about giving you permission to listen to your body and your gut. Deepak Chopra says, "The body's wisdom is a good entry point into the hidden dimensions of life…"

It's always a challenge to express Deepak Chopra's highly intelligent work in my silly-girlish way so forgive me for this simplicity:

In <u>The Book of Secrets</u>, Chopra reveals discoveries made about the human immune and digestive system. In a nut shell, **the brain isn't the only thinking organ in your body**. Other cells float around your body (outside the brain) helping you make smart decisions.

When you feel your belly flip, flop, and sense things around you... it truly is in a 'thinking' way. Your stomach is giving you information about the world around you. Deepak Chopra says, **"The stomach's reactions are just as reliable as the brain's thoughts, and just as intricate."** So the adage about a "gut reaction" is actually a glimpse into the intelligence of your body as a valid, 'thinking' source of information.

In simple stiletto terms, trust yourself!!! Feel your way! Get confirmation from the depths of your body that analyzes everything around you without over thinking it. How cool is that?!!!

Exercise

Tap into this feeling place in your body by letting go of your mind and opening up your heart.

- Make friends with an inanimate object. Maybe it's your journal, a sacred object, or even your car. Gently put your hand on it and feel as if your energy is flowing into the object. Speak your feelings and what you wish for it. Feel the space in your body that begins to connect with this object.

- Take time to marvel the many mysteries of the world. Read the first chapter of Deepak Chopra's <u>The Book of Secrets: Unlocking the Hidden Dimensions of Your Life</u>. Do the exercise "Accident or Intelligence." Ponder the magic and mystery of life without your brain asking all the *whos, whats, wheres, whens* and *whys*. Soak in the magical energy in the universe.

- Find a flower. Enjoy it. Pet it. Take in the beauty of the colors. Feel the softness of a petal against your cheek. Imagine how it felt as it grew from a seedling into a blossom and then passed its joy on to the world.

- Look into the eyes of toddler or very young child. See pure life and curiosity - untainted. Their brain hasn't taught them insecurity and fear yet. Everything is new and marvelous. You were once wonderfully open and curious too!

> *"...swim far out beyond shallow waters, plunge deep into yourself,*
> *and search patiently until the pearl beyond price is found."*

Deepak Chopra

The Treasure Hunt

What if…

First thing this morning, right when you popped out of bed, you found a little yellow post-it note stuck on your bathroom mirror. One word was scribbled on it. You smiled and instantly recognized this very familiar word but didn't (in that instant) realize its true power and how it could transform your life.

You turned the note over and on the back was a treasure map "X" marking the spot. The buried treasure was instructions to easily incorporate more of this magical little word in your life. You think to yourself, "Adding a little more in my life is no big thing. After all, it was probably the second noise that squeaked out of me as a baby."

In fact, you've probably used this healing method every single day of your life without even thinking about it. It comes as natural to you as blinking. It's as much fun as a long-overdue chat with one of your dearest friends, as cheap as **FREE**, as good for you as a 15-minute workout, yet as vital as the air you breathe. You glance again… it says "The Laughter Treasure Map."

Laughter is the no-cost, no-effort, super-simple, fabulously fun, overnight solution to happier, healthier, better living. American scientific and medical journals have cited the medical and psychological benefits of laughter:

- Heals your pain.
- Reduces your stress.
- Helps you sleep like a baby.
- Diffuses tension in difficult situations.
- Boosts your immunity.
- Fosters creativity.
- Multiplies your productivity.
- Extends your life.
- Expands your point of view.
- Bonds you to others.
- Increases your charm and charisma.
- Makes you feel happier.
- Helps you live in the moment.

With so much to gain and absolutely nothing to lose, are you ready for your "Laughing Treasure?" Every laugh you add to your life will proportionately increase the amount of joy and happiness you radiate – from the fresh air mountaintops or the cityscape rooftops!

Wrap yourself in a humorous perspective using one or all of these laughter inducing techniques taught by Cherie Kerr, founder of ExecuProv (www.execuprov.com) and author of seven other brilliant little books that will give you more laughter tips, tools, and exercises so you can fill your days with snickers, snorts, and shouts!

Exercise

- While driving in the car (and paying careful attention to the road) describe something gigantic. Maybe it's the biggest cell phone, coffee maker, or birthday card in the world!

- Play the "Remember when…" game with someone. Take turns going back and forth (or around in a circle for more than 2 people) as fast as you can "remembering when." Giggle about your earlier years, youthful naivety, and crazy past… and look how far you've come!

- Pretend you are an odd character (a cowgirl stuck in New York City for the first time trying to lasso a cab or a tourist from another planet documenting the odd things these Earth creatures do) and play it up throughout the day.

- When you recount stories from your day give them a punchy point, a profound lesson, and finish off with a big bang! Let others laugh with you.

- Watch funny things people do (on TV, out shopping, or in long lines) and put yourself in their shoes.

- Play a round of charades after dinner.

- Rent funny movies.

- Get a silly joke book or start your own by logging all the funny things people say throughout the day.

- Surround yourself with people who have wonderful senses of humor.

- Watch Comedy Central or live Improv.

- Break out of your shell, put on your stilettos, and be super silly for 10 seconds!

"The most wasted of all days
is one without laughter."

E E Cummings

Energetic And Comedic Antidotes

The brilliance of humor and laughter can make standing on your stilettos almost effortless. I'm telling you… humor will slice through the thickest tension, give you a fresh perspective, and even make you feel better on the worst 'bad hair day.'

In the past when I faced a problem or frustration, I would immediately go to this really serious and determined place, squint my eyes, and sternly focus… focus… FOCUS… searching my brain for some solution.

I realized my stern approach was more of a hindrance than a help. I wanted a new option to solve problems. I wanted to be one of those people who could burst out with spontaneous and light expression and lighten everyone's mood – and change my own energy to see possibilities instead of trials and tribulations.

I didn't do anything at first except think about it. Then, naturally, I found myself saying a mantra of sorts. I repeated it more than 10 times a day. I'd march around saying, "I solve problems with humor." I didn't know what exactly was going to happen, but I was determined and hoping for the best.

Just a couple months later, I very 'unexpectedly' and by total chance met Cherie Kerr, a founding member of the world famous L.A. Groundlings and founder of the California based, O.C. Crazies. Although I had no idea what I was getting myself into, I trusted her showed up for my first Improv class.

It changed my life! To this day you'll hear me chant Cherie's mantra, "Improv is sorda like all the lessons we should have learned when we were in kindergarten." Working with her and performing with the classy and sassy O.C. Crazies crew taught me how to solve problems with humor – and it wasn't half as tough as I expected.

I figured out pretty quickly that every time I was in my head trying to be witty, funny, or smart… the scene just bombed! The second I lived in the moment on stage, forgot about everything else, and reacted intuitively, the audience laughed and the scene was a success. The first time it happened, I remember hearing the audience laugh and I hadn't said anything funny at all. I wondered, "Why are they laughing?" My mind flashed to – my zipper is down – or – there's someone behind me doing something funny. I didn't realize how truly funny pure emotion, energy, action, and reaction could be.

Think of a time you watched a child in play and felt yourself smiling or laughing out loud. The child wasn't trying to be funny at first. It was the pure innocence and raw emotion that put a smile on your face.

Let humor be your guiding light. Take Miss Cherie's words and how-to instructions to heart. And, if you absolutely must have more quick tips ways to giggle and inject humor into your life everyday, pick up her new book *Funny Business: How To Make* <u>You</u> *Laugh On the Job Every Day*.

Let go. Laugh a little and remember you don't have to take life so seriously. Have some fun. Give up some of the stuff called "control." Life is Improv... ever changing.

Exercise

- Create a healing and heartfelt mantra to add more laughter into your life.

- Call someone who is lighthearted and energetic. Let yourself get swept up in their emotion and forget about everything else for a period of time.

> **Silly Theme** *I visualized you shouting from the rooftops with your arms in the air and your skirt flippin' in the wind before I ever named this book. Everything I wrote tied in to that brilliant rooftop energy. Each exercise would allow you to climb a little higher, feel a little freer, and gracefully skip in your stilettos shouting praises of self-love. That's the perspective I kept close to my heart as I continued to write to you and share these experiences.*

- Give your day a silly theme or create a powerful visual. Talk about daily activities and experiences in the context of that theme.

Use laughter and humor to feel connected to the moment... to the happiness and joy you desire in your life. When you live in the moment brilliant, fun, and creative solutions will stream out of you and fill your life with joy and success.

> *"At the height of laughter, the universe is flung into a kaleidoscope of new possibilities."*
>
> Jean Houston

Solve Problems With Humor

Laughter could become your most powerful secret weapon. Even though it's powerful, it's anything but dangerous. Just don't dare travel anywhere without it.

I explained how I confronted new challenges and situations – with incredible concentration and determination to get my answers. Deep in thought, analyzing every option, solution, and possible way to dig myself out of the predicament... I focused intently.

Many people solve problems by putting more tension on them instead of less. But your most brilliant solutions usually come when you are relaxing, laughing... when you are free to step away, take a new perspective, smile and see all the possibilities.

I encourage you to play a lot, laugh a lot, and find more ways to improvise new solutions in your life. It's the best way to add more joy, happiness, and peace into your life and your work. Give yourself crazy options. Take on a silly and sassy attitude. Value and call on your sense of humor when things go awry.

If a problem comes up try a new approach to solve it. Let your first response come straight from your intuition and heart. Let your head take a vacation. I try to let my first reaction be delightful wit. I've even practiced a couple phrases so they flow naturally out of me when I'm in a stressful situation.

"Ease, please!"

"I have a sneaky suspicion this will be funny soon."

"Permanecen sentado por favor."

Or try a famous line from the television sitcom "Different Strokes." Arnold perpetually asks, "Whatchoo talking about Willis?"

Throw out the rigid standards of how you approach new information. What feels right? Silly or funny in a helping way?

Instead of reacting immediately or using the same methods you used in the past, be open to new solutions and resolutions. See if humor can be infused and persevere until joy gets the job done!

Exercise

- Pick a super hero. What would he or she do to solve your problem? What crazy super power would come in handy? The lightness will not only make you giggle, but you'll have a more clear and creative mind to solve your problems.

- What would Oprah tell you if you were a guest on her show? Or is the problem so trivial you wouldn't even make it to the green room? What's the official call? Should you be so concerned about it?

- Create a silly phrase you can fall back on instead of letting vulgarities fly.

- Call a friend and vent. Start by laughing and saying, "I am so stinking happy I learned this lesson today..." It doesn't matter how bummed, angry, or mad you are in the moment, keep appreciating the beauty of the lesson and how much worse it could have been.

Infuse joy and humor into everything you do! If it will be funny later, it's funny now.

> *"Humor is a serious thing.*
> *I like to think of it as one*
> *of our greatest earliest natural resources,*
> *which must be preserved at all cost."*

James Thurber

Funny Facts For Girls Who Giggle

- It takes 42 muscles to frown and only 7 to smile.
- Children laugh about 450 times a day and adults laugh only 15 times per day.
- Laughter increases pain tolerance.
- Every time you laugh you exercise 17 different muscles in your face.
- People hardly ever laugh when they are by themselves.
- Laughing 100 times is equivalent to 15 minutes on an exercise bike.
- Laughter consists of odd variations and short vowel like notes repeated every 210 milliseconds.
- Laughter can be the "ha-ha-ha" type or the "ho-ho-ho" type but not a mixture of both.

> *"Good humor is one of the best articles*
> *of dress one can wear in society."*

William Makepeace Thackeray

PASSION AND PURPOSE

Small & Personal Passions

The world is bursting with purpose and passion. You've got it too! And chances are there are glimpses of it around you right now. I'm willing to bet you are already revealing and exposing bits and pieces of your purpose. But sometimes it feels so natural to you, you hardly see it.

An old roommate of mine is crazy for yellow. I mean over the top crazy! She could bounce from wall to wall just thinking about little balls of yellow fun in her life... and there are a lot of them in her life, let me tell you. She's got yellow everything!

- fluffy yellow blankets.
- bright yellow telephone.
- happy face pillows and bedding.
- cheery morning coffee mugs.
- warm yellow scented candles.
- yellow hats, caps, and accessories of every kind.
- big yellow bug-eye sunglasses.
- fresh yellow sunflowers.
- yellow Volkswagen Beetle car.
- even yellow books: The Persistence of Yellow.

Although I don't feel quite the same level of excitement over the color yellow, I get excited when I see yellow things out in the world and think about her. **Passion is contagious.** Just the twinkle of bright yellow sun beams and the passion I know she feels... makes me smile.

Without the attitude she takes and the perspective she makes, I would never have connected the yellow dots for myself. And as a side benefit, yellow turns out to be a very difficult color to be crabby around! Color Me Brilliant

Surround yourself with passionate people. Let your simple passions and pleasures bubble up out of you. Your passion will expose more joy, delight, and happiness everywhere you turn. It's one of the quickest and easiest ways to feel more creative, energetic, and inspired. Let passion be your ray of sunshine and stiletto strength.

Exercise

- Let your mind flutter to the simple things you love and write them down.

- Think about some of the most subtle things you take pleasure in and surround yourself with them.

- Write down three things you could do (or have been wanting to do) to fill your life with more passion.

*"The happiness of a man in this life does not consist
in the absence but in the mastery of his passions."*

Alfred Lord Tennyson

The Fire Of Your Passion

Purpose is the power and magic behind the mystery of life. It's what happens when life inexplicably falls into place.

When you are living your purpose you are propelled through life. The days feel easy and almost magical. Time feels like it is on a new continuum. When the fire of passion fills your heart, happiness ensues.

Without purpose, many people feel lost, empty, or off course. Have you ever wanted something really, really badly? Or met someone who had a single driving purpose? I love these people! You can see the fiery purpose that consumes their being. You see it in their eyes. No matter what obstacles get in the way… regardless of the struggle… the issue at hand… problems that come up… their powerful purpose plows through. They are fueled with the most unbelievable energy, motivation, inspiration, and determination to do whatever it takes.

Think about the world's finest athletes. Purpose and passion is present in every one of them. Lance Armstrong is an icon. Propelled by his passion for cycling and determination to overcome a life-threatening illness, Lance Armstrong is an inspiration and role model for dignity, courage, and survival. Under seemingly impossible odds he continues to be a hero and world champion.

Here is a man who doesn't believe in mere survival, he thrives! Untouched by what others say is 'impossible,' his passion, inner strength, and purpose propel him. The incredible thing about this spectacular athlete is that he is just like you and me. He's human. We are all capable of achieving similar accomplishments in our 'area of passion.'

Think of Lance Armstrong or any other hero you admire and let them be a resounding example of the unlimited spirit and potential available to each and every one of us.

Exercise

- What is your burning passion?
- What is your highest purpose and vision for yourself?
- What do you want to do before you leave the planet?
- What do you need to do to make your life absolutely complete?
- Think about the "why" behind all these? What drives you?

"If there is no passion in your life,
then have you really lived?
Find your passion, whatever it may be.
Become it, and let it become you
and you will find great things happen for you,
to you, and because of you."

T. Alan Armstrong

Liven Up The Mundane

Think your days need a little boost of passion? Why not liven up the mundane? Let's take an absolutely boring, unexciting, and humdrum task… like laundry. I've never met anyone who had anything exciting or passionate to say about it until I traveled to Chile.

I studied Spanish and lived with a family in Santiago for a short time. My housing included food and laundry. Mi mama would wash, line dry, fold, and stack my clothes into the most beautiful little piles you've ever seen. Never before had I seen my socks and t-shirts look so white. They sparkled. It was amazing!

I was almost excited to give her my dirty clothes. I couldn't wait to see those perfect little piles surprise me. It could have had something to do with someone actually doing my laundry for me… but the very fact that I could get so excited and passionate about a pair of clean socks shocked me.

As soon as I came home, I quickly got back into the ordinary routine of life. Laundry would pile up and I would sometimes think about mi mama.

- What was she thinking (and feeling) while she did the laundry?
- Was she filled with pride when she put her mini miracles on the edge of my bed before I came home?
- What would inspire her?
- Who else was as thrilled?
- Did she know how much I loved those perfect little piles?

Sometimes I pre-scrub stains and think about her. I smile when I pull whites out of the dryer and every sock has a mate. I neatly fold and feel a sense of satisfaction and ease putting them away. I linger in the clean fresh scent and somehow the mundane task of laundry lightens a bit.

Liven up the mundane with a positive perspective or a fresh new outlook!

Exercise

- Fulfill a function or take on a simple task today with passionate purpose.
- What passionate connections can you make to spice up the ho-hum humdrum drearies?
- What will you think about so you can work with pride and be joyful in the moment?
- How will you feel when your world sparkles?

"Enthusiasm is the greatest asset in the world."

Henry Chester

Align Your Life

Your personal values are the foundation for a very content and happy life. When you make good day-to-day choices that support your personal values, you naturally feel happy. The odd thing is few people can tell you their top five values – quickly – off the top of their head. Most people haven't taken the time to sit down, assess, and prioritize what they value most in life. But the moment you do, you will invite and allow more joy, abundance, and accomplishment into your life. You set yourself up for success!

Here are a few sample values:

Health – Wealth – Purpose

Freedom – Courage – Love

Spirituality – Faith – Self-assurance

Stability – Family – Creativity

You might look at them and think to yourself, "These are all important to me." But some rise to the top. We all prioritize them slightly differently.

Let's say your number one value is "Health" and you work in a high stress job 12 or more hours a day. You are consistently run down, stressed out, and your blood pressure is rising by the minute. Your career choice isn't supporting your number one value in life. Can you see how incredibly difficult it might be for you to be happy?

Or let's say one of your top values is "Creativity" and you continually volunteer to work over-time or help with community activities. You might find yourself not honoring your commitments or backing out at the last minute because you need more time to yourself to express your creativity. You might head up a project for a non-profit organization, but half-way through you lose interest and no longer want to do it. Even though the project is very important to you, if the choice doesn't support you living in alignment with your core values, you may feel undue stress or tension.

Begin the path of desire by assessing your values. Use them to guide your decisions and your actions so you can build a solid foundation for happiness, success, and peace of mind.

Exercise

- Brainstorm all the values important to you.
- Try to keep your list to about 15 values.
- Use this list for starters if you like.

Health	Accountability	Entertainment
Wealth	Honesty and Integrity	Enthusiasm
Purpose	Determination	Travel
Freedom	Abundance	Peace
Courage	Wisdom	Aesthetics
Love	Happiness	Success
Spirituality	Grace	Career
Faith	Interpersonal Connections	Fame and Notoriety
Self-acceptance	Respect	Adventure
Stability	Beauty	Financial Security
Family	Learning	Passion
Creativity	Self-development	Loyalty

"Try not to become a man of success.
Rather become a man of value."

Albert Einstein

A Value Proposition

Let's go deeper inside your heart to reveal the most important values you want to live by. Your truly satisfied, happy, bouncy, and successful self lies in your core values.

Each woman is dazzling and different. Trust what you know. Your values are going to be uniquely you. The only mistake you can possibly make is if you aren't sincere about what is truly important to you. Remember, all

No Supposed Tos *As you assess your values, be sure you are not considering what you are "supposed" to be. It is the way you "are" that is your truth. There is no wrong answer. Don't take on anyone else's values. Look deep inside yourself for the answers.*

the exercises are confidential. No one is going to see them or judge you. Be real. Let your wise and wonderful woman emerge!

Exercise

Here's a good way to help you discover your top five values. Give yourself some time because it could take 30 minutes or more.

- Get 15 – 20 index cards.
- Go back to the list of values that you wrote down in the last exercise and write one value on each index card.
- Pick up the first card and visualize your life with that value being the most important thing. Example: Let's say it is "Health." Picture yourself healthy and whole.
- Pick up the next card. Let's say it is "Wealth." Imagine your life in perfect financial harmony and complete abundance, but only at the sacrifice of the first value ("Health"). Example: See yourself healthy and whole, but without a dime to your name. Then reverse it see yourself with all the money in the world, but full of sickness, pain, and physical suffering.
- Go back and forth picturing your life with 100% of one value and none of the other. If you could only have one or the other, which would you choose?
- Assess which value between the two feels more important and would support you in a happier life.
- Whatever value seems more important is your number one value. That value (card) remains at the top of the stack.
- Select the next card from the stack of values. If it is "Purpose," compare it to the top value you just decided on (in this example it was either "Health" or "Wealth") Visualize "Purpose" and "Health" at the sacrifice of one another. Example: See yourself knowing your perfect purpose in life, but without any health at all. On the flip side see yourself living in perfect health but without any purpose. If you had to choose and could only have one, which would it be?
- Do the same thing for each value in the stack of cards. Every value will be directly compared to every other value, but only one at a time.
- See your top five values emerge.

This is a huge accomplishment! The first time is the most difficult. But, once you see those top five values staring at you, it's an amazing feeling of freedom.

You now have a value roadmap to make good choices. It should make decisions easier. You won't have to think as hard about the decisions you need to make. Your heart and inner wisdom aligns your actions with your values and fosters a life of harmony and deep satisfaction.

A Common Misconception

One common misconception is that values never change. Not only will your values change over time, but they will be different for different areas of your life.

Exercise

- Repeat this process once a quarter or at a minimum every year.

- Once you have your values, chart your life and see if your actions are supporting your values. Example: If your top value is "Health," look at each area of your life within the context of that value. Does your work life support all you need to feel healthy? Do your relationships foster health? Are your finances solid enough to support your health? Notice areas that might not feel right and check out what you can do to get your life in line.

- What can you can do to make good choices that are aligned with your actions?

- Try the exercise with a child and watch how they might assess their values at five, 10, or 15 years old.

 Hint: *Try not to think about more than two values while you are doing this exercise. If you try to sort out all of them at one time, it may feel overwhelming.*

"What you risk reveals what you value."

Jeanette Winterson

FROM FEAR TO PASSIONATE FLIGHT

A Little Fear In Passion

Why aren't you living with more passion?

What's holding you back?

What's stopping you?

???

You might think I'm little crazy, but there was a day my passion scared the heck out of me. I worked for a very large mutual fund company for five years. It was a fabulous company with solid values and I am still grateful for the experience to have worked there, but there was one glitch.

I worked in a cubicle on the 5th floor everyday from 8:00 a.m. – 5:00 p.m. I commuted 45 minutes to an hour each way, punched a clock, and made about 100 dials a day to connect with brokers and sell the "mutual fund of the month." I worked hard, did a good job, and became reasonably successful. After four years I was promoted…but I didn't feel happy or fulfilled.

I knew I was destined for more, but I didn't have a clue what it was. I just knew there was more. I went on day after day living the same routine. Breathing in stagnant air under the dull florescent lights, surrounded by the gray panel walls of my cubicle. I felt like a prisoner attached to my technologically enhanced headset. Not knowing when my boss would flip a switch and listen in to my calls from his office, I dreamt of fresh air, real sunshine, and a sliver of freedom.

Journaling my little heart out one day after work and searching for my purpose, I hit the jackpot. I decided I wanted to be a yoga teacher! In the most amazing and clear moment of inspiration, I (figuratively) threw on my stilettos and pranced around the room. Celebrating and wearing the biggest smile I'd felt in a long time, I felt passion and excitement coursing through my veins!

Dear Diary: Day One

> Everything seems so clear. I feel like a new woman – liberated and relieved. I want to tell the world, "I am a yoga teacher!" Hey look at me, "I know my purpose and mission!" I feel so invigorated, excited, and energized – ready to face the next phase of my life. Even my cubicle doesn't seem so suffocating. I can see the potential for my life ahead. I have more ideas and inspirations than I know what to do with. I woke up at the crack of dawn this morning… inspired and energized. I feel unstoppable, amazing, and strong. "I am a yoga teacher!"

Dear Diary: Day Twenty-One

> It's so scary and overwhelming. What if I can't do it? What if I won't do it? What if I don't make it and I'm stuck in a cubicle forever? What will people say when I fail miserably and don't do a thing I've set out to do? Or said I would? What if I don't have it in me? Can I sustain myself and actually make a living teaching yoga? What seemed so clear feels big and intimidating now.

Before that 'stiletto' moment when I saw the bright white light of my potential yoga career, I had nothing to lose. My job was disposable – it wasn't in line with my life purpose. The people at work and the clients I served didn't really get me. I had very little in common with most people. Day after day I followed rigid rules that were the farthest thing from feeling free. The job was more than a billion miles away from my heart, passion, spirit, soul, and desire.

Funny, how easy it was to justify and rationalize why I wasn't as successful or happy as I wanted to be. I figured because I didn't know my purpose in life, I had an excuse. What choice did I have? I had to pay bills and attempt to be a responsible and contributing member of society.

The second I realized what I truly loved and wanted to do with my life I had to step up. I had to take a risk. There was pressure to succeed, to be right, and do what I said I was going to do. I stared my passion in the eye and thought to myself, "Almost everyone has a dream." But when I looked around very few people had taken a risk to do something about it. It was time for me to face the music.

Exercise

Stand up and stare down your passion.

- What are you naturally good at?
- How do you enjoy supporting and inspiring others?
- How do you best serve yourself, other people, and the world?
- What do you still see yourself doing fifty years from now because your heart is in it and you love it?
- Take <u>The Rocking Chair Test</u>.

"Never continue in a job you don't enjoy.
If you're happy in what you're doing,
you'll like yourself, you'll have inner peace.
And if you have that, along with physical health,
you will have had more success than you could have possibly imagined."

Rodan of Alexandria

Protective Mechanisms Of Flight

Passion can be invigorating, but in my case you can see it was scary too. If you ever feel fear about your passion and bringing more of it into your life, get very clear about the fear you face.

Embracing your passion means some new risks may come your way – wonderful ones – but risks none the less. When you are emotionally invested in passion, fear of failure can sneak in and try to derail you. And it's even possible that the stronger your passion, the more formidable the fear may appear.

Break it down. Take passion in bite size pieces and see if you can see the difference between what is actually real and dangerous about the situation – or what is unknown F-E-A-R (False Evidence Appearing Real).

Consider someone who is afraid of heights. What is the actual danger versus what the mind perceives as dangerous? Is it the height of the cliff that frightens you? Your stomach feels queasy. Your eyeballs see how far the fall would be, but I don't think it's the cliff that is actually scaring you.

Because if you knew with 100% certainty that you could not fall – if you had some super reinforcements that would protect you, or wings to fly and land you safely, would you feel less fear?

If you knew there was a big fluffy mattress to catch you on the landing – and that your body would do a gentle, fun, flip-flop and safely catch you in the billowy mass of protection, would you be as afraid?

So the falling part isn't even the worst of it – it could actually be fun! The truly painful, scary, and potentially injury inducing fear is the moment you LAND VERY HARD! Would you agree your body hitting the pavement at 50 miles per hour is the most frightening part? The part scaring the bajeebers out of you?

Take every fear and break it down into tiny pieces. There are bad things that can actually happen and there is a bunch of other made up stuff. Your wonderfully creative brain is masterful at mixing up recipes that feel big and scary.

Find the truth and the facts. Discover the protective mechanisms of your flight.

Exercise

- What is going to keep you safe?
- What tethers do you have?
- What are your billowy cushions of delight?
- What preparations can you take and make?

"Today is a new day.
You will get out of it just what you put into it…
if you have made mistakes, even serious mistakes,
there is always another chance for you…
for this thing that we call "failure" is not the falling down,
but the staying down."

Mary Pickford

A Roadmap To Breakthrough Fear

With fluffy cushions and secure tethers to keep you safe and sound, feelings of fear in passion don't seem as big or overwhelming. You have safety nets in place so the powers of passion can rev up and whisk you to where you want to be.

When fearful voices pipe up on 'Day Twenty-One' (or whatever day it happens for you) listen and ask yourself only, "Where are the voices coming from?" Identify the places you feel additional fear. Do your best not to start a big ol' long conversation with them because the sucky part is – they often win. Prepare your safety net and embrace your passion.

Exercise

With a gust of energy and the belief that anything is possible…

- If you had no chance of failing, what would you do?
- What internal beliefs, past experiences, or perceptions are holding you back?
- What affirmations and bridge beliefs will start to change your perceptions so you can embrace your new passionate truth?

As certain I am of the fact that I was born Julie Kathleen Hunt, I am certain your passion and purpose will propel your success and happiness.

Write all that you desire (outwardly and secretly). Tell your subconscious mind you want to live your purpose. Do more than hope and pray that you will someday live with total passion. Write an affirmation Become An Affirmation Aficionado and take small action steps so you can effortlessly poise yourself on your personal rooftop pinnacle.

- What do you want?
- What most scares you?
- How does this fear serve you?

Look at moments in your life that have been filled with fear. Energetically write about them. What specifically scares you? Drill deep and keep asking whys. Create a roadmap of fear-fighting techniques you've used in the past to break through. Face your fear and run toward your passion – not away from it.

- What is directly opposite your fear?
- What will consistently propel you to face this fear and accomplish what you desire?

- How will your life be different when you courageously face your fear?
- Imagine living your life with your passion and dreams fulfilled... the fear is gone. How do you feel?

> *"The way to develop self-confidence is to do the thing you fear*
> *and get a record of successful experiences behind you."*

William Jennings Bryan

You Don't Have To Do Anything

A spectacular little book, ***You Can't Afford The Luxury Of A Negative Thought***, first introduced me to this idea. And what a marvelous, but odd thought it is, "You don't have to do anything." Soak that in for a moment. **You don't have to do anything!**

You've got choices. Remember Stephen Covey's rocks? Your life is full of fabulous choices and you get to pick and choose each and every one. No matter what you face or which options you choose, you are almost always taking a chance.

When was the last time you ate an apple? Did you look at the apple and wonder if it was sprayed with pesticides... or worry your health could be at risk? Assuming most growers use pesticides on their crops... do you stop eating all apples that aren't organic?

"Not I," said the fly! I'm going to find myself an inviting apple tree, plop down beneath it, forget about the pesticides and enjoy the crisp, fresh snap of that wonderful first bite. For me the risk is worth it. Unless you were planning to come to my house to peel, core, and bake me hot apples... maybe then I could be persuaded to wait.

How do you decide and quantify how much risk or chance you are taking? One study says that the fiber in eating an apple a day will reduce your risk of colon cancer. Another study may show that the pesticides sprayed on an apple may subject you to a seizure.

There is a flip side to every decision – more factors, benefits, and consequences than you might know what to do with. Naturally we make simple decisions like eating an apple without thinking twice. You might wash it first, wipe it on your shirt sleeve, or just dive right in, but you don't have to spend much time pondering the pros and cons.

When it comes to our list of action items some of them can feel a bit big or scary. Those will require more time – assessing, weighing, and calculating the consequences. But you don't have to do anything. Did you hear that? **You don't have to do anything!**

- Don't set yourself up for failure.
- Do what inspires, thrills, and delights you.
- Get a clear sense of the potential downside and fabulous upside.

When you know what is ahead you can make good decisions and have a greater chance of success and guarantee feelings of accomplishment (or even if it doesn't turn out quite as you had hoped, you'll learn a valuable lesson).

Breaking through fear isn't easy, but you've had hundreds of experiences in your life where it was worth it! Tap into those.

Exercise

- Determine beforehand how far you are willing to go.
- Get equipped with information to quickly and confidently decide what the risks are and if they are worth it.
- Write down the risks in black and white.
- Write a list of pros and cons.
- Listen to your intuition. Does it line up with your assessment?

You have the power, passion, strength, and skills to accomplish anything you desire. Choose wisely.

"Your life is the sum result of all the choices you make,
both consciously and unconsciously.
If you can control the process of choosing,
you can take control of all aspects of your life.
You can find the freedom that comes from being in charge of yourself."

Robert F. Bennett

Enduring Passion

Look at your passionate desires.

- Which ones rise to the top?
- Do any feel less important?
- Which ones do you feel less interested in accomplishing?
- At the end of your life – in your rocking chair – which ones will matter?

If you aren't willing to go all the way and do what it takes, then scratch it off the list and forget about it.

- Be honest with yourself.
- Let go of societal and outside pressures.
- Intimately own what you want.

You don't have to forget about it forever... just for now. Hold off until you feel bursts of passion powering through your entire body. Check in... do you feel empowered, energized, and unstoppable? If not, use the backburner for a short time. By letting go of just one thing, you clear more mind and heart space for the other unstoppable passions inside of you! You'll be on your way to accomplishing all that you desire with more drive and commitment than you may have ever experienced. Success, life, love, and happiness are on your side.

Live in honesty and make solid choices.

Exercise

- Look at situations in the past when you persevered. How did they change your life?
- And those you didn't persevere... were you as prepared and committed as you could have been?
- Did you know deep down it wasn't the right time, place, or idea?

Get in tune to all these feelings and past successes so you can see where your strength, desire, and true passion lie!

"Anything I've ever done that ultimately was worthwhile...
initially scared me to death."

Betty Bender

Prepare To Persist

Why don't most marriages work?

Coming from a single girl, I'm probably not supremely qualified to answer this question but, if you'll indulge me, I'd like to take a stab at it! With the caveat that there are probably about as many different reasons as there are divorce filings, I suppose at some point one person decides it is too difficult. There is too much work to be done, distance between the two lovers, or separation of lives and interests. One or both people end up turning and walking away.

David and I have known each other 15 years and we've dated for nearly ten. The first year was crazy difficult! And here I thought it was supposed to be all rosy. Silly me.

It was icky! The second my feelings got hurt or insecurities crept up, I wanted to bolt, run, and escape from it all. I'd usually sigh and say, "I'm so tired of this," and head for the door (or the car). Finally one day David said, "Julie, every time I hear you say 'I'm tired'… I feel like you are going to walk out."

And in all honesty, I was.

Tight chest, quivering lips, and soaked eyes I looked out to see the future of our relationship and my life. One wrong word or misunderstanding and I could see myself throwing in the towel, saying enough is enough, and walking out the door. I was so fearful of love, of getting hurt, feeling vulnerable…and being wrong. I sobbed at his little bistro table in the dining room for hours.

I knew it wasn't going to get easier. (Encouraging side note… it did!) I realized some of the pain I felt was because I did, in fact, love and adore him. I was crazy about him and all my insecurities rose to the surface. Every other relationship in my life had been easy. No fighting. No arguing. No pain. No love.

New feelings of love washed over me when I started dating David. Never had I experienced this kind of emotional investment – or vulnerability. I wasn't all that sure of what I even wanted before that moment. Then I decided. David was the perfect boy for me; the man I wanted to be with forever.

No matter how hard our relationship would get, I decided I would go all the way. Silently, in my heart, I made a commitment to marry him (unbeknownst to him at the time). I promised myself I wouldn't run, hide (for too long), or give up completely. That was the turning point in our relationship.

If you aren't willing to go all the way – with anything you desire in your life – at some difficult moment you may see your shadow, watch it stop, turn, and walk away.

Exercise

- Will you make a personal decision to persist and face the continued challenges?
- Are you willing to look at life from a different vantage point and look outside yourself with a new clarity or perspective?
- Will you carry on until the tables turn back in your favor? Because if you make a decision to persist and carry on, eventually the tide will turn.

> *"I will persist until I succeed.*
> *Always will I take another step.*
> *If that is of no avail I will take another.*
> *In truth, one step at a time is not too difficult…*
> *I know that small attempts, repeated, will complete any undertaking."*

Og Mandino

Passion, Persistence, And Perseverance

Many of the most marvelous feats of history, science, and humanity have occurred when a single person was consumed with passion and persistence. Desire so intense it overcame all obstacles. Even in the face of ridicule, judgment, and persistent failure… these men and women persisted.

One particular man always stands out to me. He was born into poverty and his mother died when he was young. He was spectacular at one thing for most of his life – failure. He successfully failed at almost everything he tried, until very late in his life.

He failed in business twice, suffered from a nervous breakdown once, and survived the death of his sweetheart. He was defeated in two legislative races, three congressional races, two senatorial races, one vice-presidential race, until he was finally elected President of the United States at age 60.

Abraham Lincoln persisted with passion.

He used every failure in his life to deepen his personal character. In my mind, the 16th president of the United States of America is the epitome of perseverance. I believe he is one of the greatest presidents this country has ever known. He used his entire being to pursue and accomplish his goals.

Failing is scary and rejection hurts. Yet both are components of success. Think about the things in your life that you worked really hard for. Recall how sweet the reward was. The more difficult the journey, the sweeter the success.

I once heard someone say the **more mistakes you encounter, the faster you are learning**. Let each and every hiccup and hurdle remind you that the prize is worth it. **View failure as just one simple lesson of what not to do.** Check off one way that didn't produce the desired effects and move quickly to a new solution. Colonel Sanders was turned down 1,009 times before someone saw the value of his Kentucky Fried Chicken recipe.

As certain as you are of your desires, let your entire being propel you forward. As you accomplish tiny bite-size bits of success, let your confidence and happiness fill every other area of your life.

Exercise

- Make a list and document all the obstacles and problems you could encounter while you are on your journey. How will approach them?

- Celebrate failure as if it was a success. You were just successful at learning one new way that won't work. That's a big Whoo-hoo!

- Change your approach and discover a better way to achieve all you desire.

- Don't go back to the options that didn't create your desired results, try new solutions.

- Tally your attempts until you succeed. You never know, someone may want to write about you someday!

- Persist until you succeed and add some fun, joy, laughter, and lightness to the process.

"Always bear in mind that your own resolution
to succeed is more important than any other."

Abraham Lincoln

You Can Be Right Or Happy

Sometimes the universe has a bigger and better plan for you. It may be hard to see some days, but I guarantee there is a ton in store for you. Much more than you or I could possibly imagine. Look for it. Look deeply and free yourself to live a happy and vibrant life!

I strongly urge you to start releasing the concerns on your mind. Because the things you fear have a very odd and sneaky way of becoming reality.

So, you can be right… or you can be happy! Which do you want to be?

Do you want let the fear of failure prove you were right all along and you couldn't do it? Or do you want to live happily and be wrong about how real the fear felt?

The wall of fear you see is not a reality. It's an illusion. Fear is so great and looming that it feels real, but it's not. And we've all got so many fears; I'm surprised we get anything done at all. Be bold. Look at the risks and weigh them out carefully. You have the power to create what you desire… and I support all of your decisions unconditionally.

Remember, you don't have to do anything you don't want to, just don't let the big, scary, false wall of fear stop you when there is something you want.

Use your unstoppable passion, determination, and drive to run toward what you want in your life and move through it. Remember fear is an illusion – your mind playing tricks. Don't let it prove you right.

Exercise

- What have you feared in the past that you busted through and found it wasn't so hard after all?

- How much more joy will you experience in your life when you release your fear and break through?

- How will you know what is good and right for you? How will you feel? Move? Walk? Behave? Talk?

"Try a thing you haven't tried before three times
— once to get over your fear, once to find out how to do it,
and a third time to find out whether you like it or not."

Virgil Thomson

Run For Your Life

Run your little heart out and seize all that you desire. Run… run… run… in the right direction, that is!

Too many times, in the face of fear, we bolt the other way. It's easy to run away from something big and scary. But, running from fear only strengthens fear. If you run away you give it power.

Remember the universal law of attraction? <u>You Are A Powerful Magnetic Attractor</u> It says you get what you focus on. If you spend time thinking about negative consequences, those thoughts can be damaging and produce a physical outcome – if you don't stop them in time. I believe the bold courageous woman inside of you is the one who can strap on a saucy pair of stilettos and run like the wind toward every desire that lives within your heart.

I used to say that I wanted to completely eliminate fear from my life. My girlfriends would laugh and tell me I was nutty. They'd try to explain that fear could propel me toward what I wanted, but I didn't see it. I couldn't see a potential positive result. In fact, when I reflected back on some of my most embarrassing, shameful, or regretful moments – fear gripped my body and took over my mind.

On my first trip to Europe, I was standing on a train platform in Germany. Our train hadn't arrived yet and we had 15 minutes until it was expected to depart. I sat on a stack of luggage while David went to get us a quick snack. While he was feeding deutsche marks to the vending machine for a stale ham sandwich, the train roared into the station 10 minutes early. Every person on the platform rushed the train. I panicked!

Five minutes later David lightheartedly reached the platform, his hands full of snacks. Of course, the train was there patiently waiting for an on-time departure. Overwhelmed with fear, uncertainty, and anger, I believed the train was going to leave early. I lost it and blamed him for the whole thing.

Completely humiliated, I learned a powerful lesson about fear. I saw how a single illusion in my mind sent my mouth and blood pressure racing a million miles an hour. It made me look at how I would handle fear in the future and I came up with a strategy to "use fear under fire." I now attempt to use fear as a motivator to practice under pressure – be calm, loving, strong, and positive. Don't get me wrong, I can still freak out – but a lot less often.

The psychology of fear is half the battle. My goal now is not to eliminate fear, but to use it to my advantage. Use it as a positive influence to be the incredibly calm, positive woman that I know I can be. I hope to always run toward the lesson and embrace the challenge of managing fear so I can be a better friend, woman, and human.

Use the energy, excitement, momentum and thrill of fear that seems dangerous to stay cool, calm, and collected. Be a role model in difficult situations.

- Run toward what you want in your life.
- Stay focused and move through uncomfortable feelings.
- Remind yourself fear is an illusion. It is your mind playing tricks.
- Ask yourself what you are truly fearful of. Put it in perspective.
- Breathe steadily and rhythmically.
- Build familiarity with fear. Learn and study what you are afraid of. Facts eliminate some of the mystery behind fear.
- Stay healthy and be well rested. (You probably wouldn't try a new extreme sport without proper rest. Life is an extreme sport!)

Feel the excitement, challenge, and exhilaration of fearful situations. Let your natural strengths propel you toward freedom, independence, and the change you desire.

"The difference between the impossible and the possible lies in determination."

Tommy Lasorda

STEP INTO ACTION

The Freedom Of Movement

Are you ready to move... shake, rattle, and roll?! Yes, me... I am! Will you whisk me away with you? There is something about movement and action that feels so incredible to me.

I realized it one day driving to my Grandma's house. It was the most beautiful Saturday afternoon. I was driving with the top down. No hurry. Plenty of time. Music thumpin'. 78 degrees. Cumulus clouds in the sky. Happy as a clam 'til traffic stopped and all momentum was gone.

WELCOME TO CALIFORNIA

I was at a stand still on the 405. The sun on my face and my favorite CD still didn't distract me enough from feeling fussy and antsy. I looked up ahead. Next for my phone. Then, I practically panicked. I felt so trapped! No where to go.

In a jiffy, the traffic jam loosened up. My stilettos pressed down on the accelerator... 20... 30... then 45 miles per hour. I was big again!

You know I'm a goof ball... but I share this because it was the first time I ever felt (or realized at least) the physical sensation of the freedom of movement.

Exercise
- Be aware of your body and physical movements. What kind of actions or movements feel right and good to you?
- When you feel happy and energetic, how do you move your body? What hand gestures do you use? Facial expressions? Your posture?
- Experiment and make big or exaggerated gestures throughout the day. Give big hugs. Take long, confident strides. Do one task at a time with your full energy, mind, heart and both hands in on the activity.

Any time your energy feels low – stifled – or stuck… get up!

- Sit up tall.
- Stand up straight.
- Talk about someone or something you love a LOT. (Or make up a pet peeve story. This is a great way to generate lots of energy. Laugh about it when you are done!)
- Take a quick walk.
- Move your limbs.
- Shake out your arms.
- Roll up on your tippy-toes.
- Get your bottom shakin'.
- Give your body a jolt!

Feeling stuck and then effortlessly being released out into the world (or more realistically the 405 highway) made me think seriously about happiness, purpose, passion, and productivity. For me the movement created freedom and happiness. Let your life be filled with wonderful actions that propel you forward.

"Freedom is the oxygen of the soul."

Moshe Dayan

Nothing Happens Without A Thought

Your heart and soul drives your passion. Then your marvelous mind starts to move your body so your sassy stilettos will march one foot in front of the other. Without your brain in on the action, nothing much is going to happen. Even if you feel the urge to go to the bathroom your brain has to say, "Bladder alert." Then, you'll get up and mosey (or in my case run) to the bathroom.

If you had to wake up tomorrow, an hour earlier than normal, first your brain would have to process and think about it. Then, you'd take a physical action to set the alarm and (hopefully) wake up right on time when it buzzes tomorrow morning.

Even new life starts as a thought. The adage goes, "You were just a twinkle in your father's eye."

John-Roger and Peter McWilliams couldn't have said it better in ***You Can't Afford The Luxury Of A Negative Thought***... maybe not overnight, but eventually the energy and thoughts you focus on will produce physical results in your life. Negative thoughts produce negative results and positive thoughts produce positive ones. Violà!

(psssst... every word in ***You Can't Afford The Luxury Of A Negative Thought*** is worth reading!)

When passion is coursing through your veins, positive thoughts are almost effortless. Think about a time when you couldn't stop thinking about the excitement of a new relationship, project, or activity. Where was your mind? How did you get anything else done? Were your conversations with others consumed with the thrill of this new adventure? Did your mind continually drift off, dream, and think deeply about it?

- You saw the potential.
- Visualized new opportunities.
- Dreamt up marvelous possibilities.

Spontaneously you created a happy place in your mind encouraging creativity and wonderful aspirations. Then positive actions spilled out of you, naturally and effortlessly. Change your life (or your day) any time you want just by thinking about it.

Exercise

Turn ideas into reality.

- Write three very small and simple desires you would like to experience in your life.
- Visualize these areas in the most delightful, pleasant, and pleasing way possible.
- See yourself taking a small and easy action that will take you closer to your optimal state.
- Walk around as if this ideal is your reality today. Pretend it is true.
- Think, speak, act, and behave as if that desire has been fulfilled.

> *"Positive thoughts (joy, happiness, fulfillment, achievement, worthiness) have positive results (enthusiasm, calm, well-being, ease, energy, love). Negative thoughts (judgment, unworthiness, mistrust, resentment, fear) produce negative results (tension, anxiety, alienation, anger, fatigue)."*
>
> Peter McWilliams and John-Roger

Small And Steady Wins The Race

More happiness, abundance, creativity, love, health, and even more peace of mind come with beautiful and small movements of action.

Before you get all riled up or feel like you have to 'do' something, sit back for a moment and relax. Our lives have become oh-so busy that when someone says, "You have to do something," it's easy to feel a little excited as you worry about the other 427 things on your to-do list. So if you are skeptical and reluctant to add one more thing to the list, I hear you!

How about if we accept a belief that all action should be fun and inspiring? Not big and overwhelming, just itty-bitty teeny-tiny steps that allow you to feel wonderful and encouraged as you move in the right direction. You don't have to go out and change the world all at once — like sometimes I know you want to do! Keep it small. Because if you try to tackle it all at once chances are you'll get burnt-out, bored, or find something more interesting to do. It's not a matter of if, but when.

So grab your comfiest pair of shoes. The ones you adore. **Small baby steps will give you the freedom of movement and action without having to take everything in stride all at once.** Forget about the feat of scaling the 50 story high-rise today! Let's just saunter out to the balcony for a sip of fresh air and a big toe baby step to see what marvels await you.

Start to feel your energy rising and the possibilities bubbling. Feel the power you have to create change in your life. Find a small and wonderful action that suits your style. As you do the next exercise, send or share your notes with a friend (or me!). Let someone in on your action plan. Exchange all the tiny (and fun) actions that have the potential to completely realign your life and your happiness!

Exercise

Take small, playful, and meaningful actions.

- Plan out a week of easy actions (one tiny action per day) that would alleviate some stress or add a splash of sunshine to your home or work life.

- Share them with a friend or look for a buddy that you can play with and hold each other accountable. (I'm here too! Email: julie@shesite.com)

- Look at them with a special and encouraging someone and brainstorm ways to make it even more fun or easier to accomplish.

Choose small actions that will take you closer to your passion, purpose, and goals. Write them in your journal now if you haven't already. Visualize happiness moving toward you with every action you wrote down. See yourself with little effort making luxurious stiletto strides.

Celebrate your progress and each and every movement, even if it doesn't take you exactly where you expected to be. Ask yourself along the way, "How am I beginning to feel?"

"What we call results are beginnings."

Ralph Waldo Emerson

Your Brain On Big

Here is your brain on BIG: Arghhhhhhhhh!

Here is your brain in action: **Take it on, baby!**

Your brain thinks big. And that's good. But sometimes it leans toward projects instead of actions. Look back at the last exercise and what you committed to do.

- How many did you check off? Why? Or why not?

(If little time has passed, then look at the list every day for the next seven days. Try to complete one action every day.)

- What actions are left after seven days? Were you a star performer? Did you send your action items to someone else, for their input? Hooray you! Or... not?

Send 'em to me now. We still have time. And when you do send them, take a little guess about what I might say. Typically, my response doesn't change all that much, even after seeing lots and lots of action steps, I usually repeat the definition of a "baby step" and ask...

Exercise

- How can you break the items into smaller and smaller actions?
- What could you do in two minutes on that one action to move yourself forward?
- What could you do to have more fun doing them?

Consider the beauty and benefits of tiny actions. How darn good are you going to feel when you get to check off all those little boxes and create joy and happiness in your life?

You might have lots of steam right now, but in 3 – 4 – 6 – 8 weeks how will you feel? Will you be as determined as ever to forge ahead and do whatever it takes? Sometimes we need a little push start at the beginning (or an extra push during the process to get us back on track) Hence: The Two Minute Miracle

> *"There is a soul force in the Universe,*
> *which if we permit it will flow through us*
> *and produce miraculous results."*
>
> Mahatma Gandhi

The Two Minute Miracle

Can you feel the momentum beginning to take hold?

Your body is fueled with fabulous energy. I see you are wearing even taller heels these days! You have plenty of steam right now, but how will you sustain this blissful energy and happiness? How will you guarantee it's not just a rah-rah session of get-up-and-go that's likely to disappear as quickly as it came?

While I was launching SHE (www.shesite.com) and working with my coach, Terri Levine, I had written and committed to accomplish five action items within the next week. Very deliberately, I selected and wrote out actions that would be challenging, yet simple and fun enough so I could get them done. I wanted to see progression and feel a sense of accomplishment. Two weeks later I still hadn't accomplished three of the five things. And since I'm typically a "doer," I beat myself up wondering why I couldn't fulfill on my promise to myself.

Terri told me to set my computer timer and brace myself for a two-minute marathon of simple actions. I chose, what I thought was the easiest one, "Buy Domain Name." With my credit card in hand, I raced to a site where I could purchase domain names. The only thing I got was a "thunk" on the head when I slammed into the brick wall in front of me. I realized instantly that what I had written down was a project, not a task.

I needed to complete more than 25 tasks before I could purchase the domain name. I hadn't even named the company yet. I realized there were even projects within projects like "Research Business Name Options" and "File Fictious Business Permit." No wonder I wasn't getting anything done. I hardly knew where to start.

Break up your leftover actions into 3–5 smaller action items. Let's take a common example, say "Plan a Vacation."

It seems simple enough, but who plans a vacation in a day? Planning a vacation, again, is more of a project – not an action. So when you see "Plan a Vacation" come up on your list of things to do, it's not surprising that your brain freezes, fries, or avoids it altogether. You subconsciously avoid or check out because the task is so big. You can't accomplish it in one day.

Use the Two Minute Miracle approach and break up your vacation project into smaller action items. For example:

- Ask your best friend for her favorite travel spots.

- Buy *Budget Travel* at the grocery store's newsstand.

- Log on to the computer for two minutes and look at Expedia travel packages.

- Get out the phone book and write down the name and phone number of one travel agency.

- Call one travel agency and ask an agent to mail you a brochure.

Can you see how you could go on and on breaking down this list of easy actions? These tiny actions hopefully seem more doable and will eventually lead to a fabulous summer soirée.

Big projects don't facilitate easy movement. Make your movements so swift and simple that they are practically automatic. Then you'll find yourself almost to the top of the roofline enjoying a breathtaking view (or vacation)!

Exercise

- Think about things you've wanted to accomplish in your life.

- What small actions could you take today to move forward? Hint: it can be as simple as telling a friend… or even sharing it with me!

- Use a Two Minute Miracle to move it! Get an egg timer and flip! For two minutes, work to get unstuck from an action item that is holding you back (or you don't seem to be getting around to). Committing to just two tiny minutes every day means soon you can enjoy BIG accomplishments!

93

- Do silly stuff to inspire you to action. Find a friend you can giggle with or zoom to the latte line for a shot of espresso. If you prefer natural energy, infuse the room with the scent of peppermint and you'll feel more alert.

> *"Change is the end result of all true learning.*
> *Change involves three things:*
> *First, dissatisfaction with self — a felt void or need;*
> *second, a decision to change — to fill the void or need;*
> *and third, a conscious dedication to the process*
> *of growth and change — the willful act of making the change;*
> *Doing Something."*

Ease Off Perfectionism

Now, just hold your horses!

What the heck are you waiting for sweet girl? Any idea what's stopping' or stalling you? Me neither! You have passion bursting and opportunities a' waiting. I'm guessing there is something on your mind you'd like to accomplish… some passion bubbling under the surface.

Don't let any more time pass by. There is so much joy, love, excitement, self-satisfaction, and gratification you are going to feel on this journey. But maybe… just maybe… you desire it so much that you want everything to be perfect. Hmmm. To that I say, nutin' … and I mean N-O-T-H-I-N-G will ever be perfect. And that's a beautiful thing.

I could go on for days about the 'flaws' of perfectionism. In a nutshell, if you are going to wait for the stars to align you will miss out on oodles of dreamy nights. Do what you please. Start small if it is something new. Invite friends over, go out, stay in, take a break, talk a million miles an hour, change up your inside or your outside, tell someone you dig them, ask for help, clear up a mix-up, express yourself authentically, be wildly creative, or just curl up and get cozy. But don't hesitate.

There will always be more stuff to do, lessons to learn, and things unraveling in front of you. I guarantee it! Waiting is for sissies.

But I'll admit I'm guilty of it, too! This information is so challenging for me to send to you. I want it to come in the most brilliant way. I want you to soak up every word. I want it to be meaningful, helpful, and useful. I want it to be beautiful. Text isn't half as much fun without colors, patterns, textures, and a wonderful design. I want you to feel my heart, passion, and most of all, my belief in you. I believe in you!

This book will never be perfect. Never. I can tweak forever and freak out all night because a hundred little words and phrases aren't just right! So, I really have only two choices: Wait until it's perfect and risk never letting you taste these morsels of self-knowledge and delight, or let it all out right now so you can soak it in… flaws and all!

I believe this book will touch every woman who is meant to read it. And, you're right! It's not going to be for everyone. That's ok too! But my intentions are pure. I can't please everyone all the time. If I begin to worry about what some people will think or say, or if I keep all this information buried in the files of my computer, then I'm not doing all I possibly can to touch women in the world and live my truth. As difficult as it was to create a deadline and send this to you now, I had to do it. I beg you to take a leap into the world and trust one principle:

Execution Before Perfection

You have amazing, brilliant talents, desires, and goals bubbling up inside of you. There is no better time than the present to let them find their way to the surface and shine.

Exercise

<u>Are You A Perfectionist?</u>

Rank yourself on a scale from 1-5. (1 – No, that's not a fit for me; 5 – Yes, that's me to a tee!)

- Do you have trouble making decisions?
- Do you spend more time planning and less time doing?
- Do you have lots of systems and ways of doing things that you enforce with others at work or home?
- Do you carry excessive guilt?
- Are you troubled when you have to leave things to do later?
- Do you stress yourself out when you make a commitment, always coming through even when you could call, postpone, or alter the commitment?

- Is your free time highly organized, scheduled in advance, and very well planned?

- Do you enjoy competitive games or sports only when you are the champion?

- Do you feel let down often because you've set unrealistically high expectations?

- Are you afraid of people seeing your flaws or finding out you're human, too?

- Will you think about what needs to be done, even when you've promised yourself you'll let it go?

- When you have done your best, but not performed as well as you would have hoped, do you continue to beat yourself up?

Let go of some of the demands you put on yourself. No one else is as hard on you as you are. Don't miss your moment. Seize the opportunity. Sure it may not be perfect, but it will be perfectly you!

> *"Every morning is a fresh beginning.*
> *Every day is the world made new.*
> *Today is a new day. Today is my world made new.*
> *I have lived all my life up to this moment, to come to this day.*
> *This moment – this day – is as good as any moment in all eternity.*
> *I shall make of this day*
> *– each moment of this day –*
> *a heaven on earth.*
> *This is my day of opportunity."*

Dan Custer

To Hesitate Or Not To Hesitate

What's the downside? What do you have to lose? Are you hesitating for a reason? Or because fear is poking its ugly head and appearing to you as real?

There will always be new information to learn… something else to do… more ways to grow… extra progress to make… and positive change to seek. Why wait, my little snicker doodle?

Why hesitate?

All that we lack could and should be a gentle reminder of how much more room there is to live and grow. My personal mantra is: "I am always learning and growing in a playful, positive, and creative way."

No matter how bad, frustrating, or overwhelming a situation seems, perceive it as a lesson, as something worth learning. Ask yourself what is the lesson in this? When you seek knowledge you build up the courage to get through anything.

Where will you be the minute you stop learning, or come to the end of your rope?

Don't let go of the rope! Let go of the outcome. Don't wait for the someday. Revisit what you truly want.

- What do you want?
- What's your motive?
- What is your intention?
- What is your passionate desire?
- What activities could keep your interest forever?

Exercise

Look at a few areas in your life that you are still "waiting for."

- Write down every "someday" … "one day" … and "sooner or later" that you think you'll "get around to."
- Why are you hesitating? What is the worst thing that can happen?
- What could you do today to play, enjoy, flitter to and fro, and make it more fun?
- How will you know when you are ready?
- What will you do to move forward and feel free in the flow of action?

You are beautiful, amazing, and you are enough. Know you have unconditional acceptance from another woman (that's me!) and I promise to share your enthusiasm when you succeed and not be critical of the mistakes along the way. We all make the same (or, at least similar) mistakes. And if we haven't, then that's just because they are right around the corner waiting for us to face them. So while it's just you and me, just the two of us, and your journal...

- See blemishes as beauty!
- Movement as magnificent.
- Feel full of pride and progress even if it's not perfect!
- Step up and step out.
- Reveal yourself.
- Strut your stuff.
- Show yourself off!

And thanks, sweet girl, for allowing me to be me... with my funky flaws, whacked-out words, ways, and grammar. We're all on this wonderful journey together.

"How many cares one loses when one decides
not to be something but to be someone."

Coco Chanel

Incapacitated By Indecisiveness

How much in your life have you already missed out on because you waited to make a decision? Decisions factor powerfully into your ultimate happiness. Think for just a second about how miraculous one decision can be.

- Reflect back to a time when one small decision changed your life.

When you embrace new decisions that feel good to you, you instantly move yourself forward toward amazing things! Don't let yourself get caught in a trap of indecisiveness.

Indecisiveness is an invitation for fear and irritation to come over to your house for a visit. Have you ever felt the weight of the world fall away the second you made a decision, even if it was a really difficult one? Even if you were uncertain about the outcome, the certainty of a decision is solid and grounding.

Once you make a choice, a lot of lingering stress disappears. Gone. Zap! You just bought lots of space and energy to take some mini movements to move you toward what you want, instead of wondering which direction you want to go. I pinky promise that once you make a decision and move forward – **the actions never turn out as scary as you might have thought**.

Start with baby steps that feel right, good, and are at just your speed. Get up the confidence and momentum you need to succeed. Then you'll be able to enthusiastically plow through the rest of the fears. What's the result? It's the unstoppable you doing a little tap dance on the rooftops. Put on those stilettos and shout it out!

Make good decisions and let your mind rest with ease. **Use your energy to act instead of worry about what could, should, or would happen.**

Exercise

Helpful hints to make wise, powerful decisions:

- Set an intention to make good decisions that support your life.
- Look at the end goal and ask yourself which choice best guides you to where you want to go?
- Weigh the options and consider the best and worst case scenarios.
- If you feel stuck, use my "By the Way" formula. All things being equal, will the action "better" your life (improve the situation) or slightly "worsen" it? Rarely does a decision have absolutely zero affect. If it truly makes no difference, then celebrate what an easy choice it is. (Hint: selecting a restaurant for dinner is usually relatively neutral. Pick a place and go.)
- If it's a big decision, walk away and don't think about it... or wait 24 hours to make your final decision.
- Talk about the decision with one person you trust. While you hear yourself talk, it may bring incredible clarity to know if you are, indeed, making the right decision.
- Make a decision quickly and then change your mind slowly.

Every decision you make makes you stronger and prepares you to make even better choices in the future. Consider asking yourself:

- What will I learn?
- How will the choice help me grow?
- Is the decision an inspiring one that feels right for me?
- Will it be fun?

"In my analysis of several hundred people who had accumulated fortunes well beyond the million-dollar mark...
every one of them had the habit of reaching decisions promptly and of changing these decisions slowly...
People who fail to accumulate money, without exception, have the habit of reaching decisions, if at all, very slowly..."

Napoleon Hill, Think & Grow Rich

BE TRUE TO YOU

I ❤ Me

When was the last time you were the most important thing in the whole wide world… just you?

Head

Heart

Spirit

Mind

Brilliant Body

Just Pure You!

When was the last time the only thing that mattered started at the tip-top of your head and ran to the soulful stilettos grounded beneath your feet – and, of course, included all the great stuff inside and in between? When was the last time you were so engrossed in *you*, you forgot about everyone else and what they needed? Your mind was at ease. Drifting. Simple. Lovely. Almost empty?

Ok? Maybe for just a second? A nanosecond? Well, I think I've made my point. One of the most awesome lessons you can embrace is to walk away from work, responsibility, obligations, and duties… and take time out just for you! *Truly.*

I suspect you doubt me. Maybe you think I don't understand your situation or how busy you are. But hear me when I say, **"When you disregard your sense of self, overwork your body, discount your beauty, ignore your freedom, and pay so little attention to yourself you know more about the snail status on the driveway, you are giving *away* your happiness and joy."** I don't believe you will ever be truly happy if you exclude or don't care for yourself. (p.s. caring for yourself doesn't include mandatory family outings or shaving your legs in the shower).

If you don't put yourself first, eventually the craziness of life will catch up with you. You'll feel tired, spent, and worn out. You've been there! Maybe you're there right now. Are you?

The secret to a balanced and happy life is to ease off and step away on a regular basis. No matter if you need to or not. Stopping is one of the hardest things I've ever done.

Responsibilities never seem to stop tugging. Obligations keep sneaking in without me even realizing it. Emergencies flare up more quickly than an Italian's hot temper. But constant work without play and relaxation eventually creates stress, self criticism, loss of vital energy, and poor health. In order to live vibrantly you must h-e-a-r-t you!

Whenever you feel too pressured, short of time, or like people around you are tugging at you, know that if you give in everyone will suffer. Your effectiveness, joy, creativity, courage, and productivity will dwindle away… and you won't be able to show up on the rooftops as vibrantly and joyfully as you were meant to.

Say, "Enough is enough! Time to stop. Time to play!" I say it's time to give yourself permission to goof off before you finish your work. Life is just too short to let the 'shoulds' get in the way of your living! I vote you put yourself first today and put the rest of the 'shoulds' in check.

Exercise

Check in the 'shoulds.'

- Muster up the strength and courage to say "No!"
- Put up boundaries that support what you need.
- Live your passion and take two minutes to learn more about something you've always wanted to do, but never thought you had time for.
- Pamper yourself with simple Home Spa Tips at www.shesite.com.

> *"You have to decide what your highest priorities*
> *are and have the courage*
> *– pleasantly, smilingly, nonapologetically –*
> *to say 'no' to other things.*
> *And the way you do that is by having*
> *a bigger 'yes' burning inside."*

Stephen Covey

Shouts Of No!

What do you dream of? What makes your heart sing and your feet tap?

There is so much more love, passion, and purpose inside of you, why are you still hiding it? Your happiness is delicately woven within your purpose and your dreams.

I know for me, I've got so many delightful dreams and inspirations flickering in my mind that sometimes it's hard to stay still and listen to just one of them. I like to think I can chew gum, roller skate, bee bop to a beat, enjoy the great outdoors, and still watch out for the cracks in the sidewalk, but one broken tooth later and I know I need to choose my priorities carefully. So I choose very carefully to do the things I love… the things I want to commit to… and only take on projects I thoroughly enjoy.

After years of being the overcommitted girl feeling stressed and disappointed in myself and disillusioned by how much I could take on at once, I collapsed. One little two letter word would have saved me, "No!"

I believe the vision for your life and your dreams will come to pass when you start using the word "No." The word "No" can liberate you and set you free!

The Word No *Quite possibly the single most underused word by women.*

Just think about how many times you dreaded fulfilling some commitment. Think about the little agreements you made. How many other times did you tell a little white lie because you didn't want to say "No?" What about all the times you didn't say it, but wanted to? Then backed out on your promise and disappointed yourself later.

There is some serious freedom in the word "No." Not only will you open up doors of opportunity, time, and free expression for you, but you'll feel a sense of confidence that is like no other. Your true, genuine, honest self will radiate!

Do you ever feel the need to say "yes" to everything? Why?

Maybe, you didn't want to be the "bad guy," hurt someone's feelings or disappoint them. But in reality, who is getting hurt? The world thinks you are an "Agreeable Sweet Pea," but you are the one suffering. You will be the one with feelings of disappointment. Use the word "No." Say it loud and feel proud that you are honoring your needs as a woman. And, it doesn't have to be a bitter, hard, cold "No." Say no with love, compassion, and understanding. My mother always said, "You can say anything you want, it's just how you say it."

As you hear a request, invitation, or summons coming on, listen for the goodness in it. There is probably a compliment, kind word, or admiring consideration implied in the request. Let's say you are invited to a party you don't want to go to. Say, "Thanks for your invitation. I love spending time with you. I'm sorry however, I'm unavailable. I'll be thinking about you and hoping all is wonderful."

Life is too short. Use the word "No."

Exercise

- Say "No," just once today. That's all.

"I'd rather say no and have said no and do say no often.
I walk away from projects if it doesn't feel right;
if it's not the right team of people pulling
in together or if the script isn't right.
It could be a great idea but the script doesn't work."

Blair Underwood

Consider the script for your life.

Integrity And Commitments

Commitments rock, but only when you feel good about them and you are truly prepared to take action and energetically follow through. <u>You Don't Have To Do Anything</u> If not, you could be setting yourself up for failure.

Take the ominous New Year's Resolutions as an example. My opinion, "HORRIBLE!" January 1st rolls around and society asks to you recognize some glaring personality or life flaw. You get to tell everyone about it. Pretend you want to fix it. Without planning, preparation, or much foresight, you plow ahead and determine this time you'll do it. Most of the time, you end up failing miserably or making only a temporary change. Statistically New Year's Resolutions just don't stick.

How's that for a bit of optimism for you? The good news is there is a very simple reason for this that will blow the doors to your success wide open every time you make a commitment or a well-thought-out New Year's Resolution.

The Brunch Table

> We're all drinking mimosas and someone says, "Hey, what's your resolution for the new year?" Around the table it goes… everyone declares their new beginnings and promises for the new year.
>
> Of course, you aren't going to pick something simple and small, even if it's important to you. You'd never say, "I promise to water and care for the house plants!" Instead you pick out something big and monumental, something that's been plaguing you for months or years. The infamous, "I promise to quit smoking" or "… lose twenty-five pounds."

Just thinking about some of my crazy resolutions that never lasted gives me incredible insight into this very topic. Will you honestly be happy, committed, and ready to successfully overcome a personal challenge just because it's the first day of the year and society says you should do it?

I think almost every person has made a resolution they didn't keep. When we don't come through on our personal commitments to ourselves we feel frustrated, disappointed, and critical. Without giving a moment's notice about what you were prepared to actually do, you make a commitment for the year.

- Every day of the year is a perfect day to choose change.
- Do it when you are ready. When you have such strong desire and motivation nothing will derail you.
- Make strong promises that fit your time frame, situation, and personal happiness plan.

Each and every day of the year, feel free to use your bright, brilliant, beautiful mind to make smart and lasting decisions.

Exercise

- Make small commitments regularly – ones you feel very sure you'll follow through on.
- Be realistic about the *whats* (what you want to accomplish) and the *whens* (in what time frame).
- Verbalize your commitments to someone you trust. Gain their support.
- Set mini and ongoing deadlines so you can adapt and adjust without getting too far off track.

Examples

- If you want to live healthier, start by taking the stairs instead of the elevator once a week.
- If you want a better relationship, try writing down three things you appreciate in your partner before you go to bed.
- If you want to remodel your home, try house plants, pillows, and paintings first.

Take tiny actions and watch them soon become good habits. Once you feel good about those actions, add another small change. Or if you didn't stick with the change don't beat yourself up, try another option that might suit you better. Small And Steady Wins The Race

Let yourself feel wonderful about your progress instead of setting yourself up for failure. That's the gorgeous stiletto girl coming out in you! Make commitments and find small ways that will allow you to feel happy and enjoy the journey.

> *"He who is most slow in making a promise*
> *is the most faithful in the performance of it."*
>
> Jean-Jacques Rousseau

Peak Life Moments

Think about some of your peak life experiences. What were you doing? Who were you with? What was happening? David and I share this little saying, "I'm having a peak life moment."

It usually happens someplace totally ordinary. I'm either with someone I adore and I feel an overwhelming feeling of love. Or, I'm all by myself and my mind is closed down from thought, interpretation or judgment... only feeling.

These moments mean more to me than any level of success, material possession, or achievement. They are the moments I live for day to day. There's nothing better than when one sneaks up on me and plows me down with love and gratitude. You might even see my eyes get a little weepy.

Yet, there are a hundred more times I just go right on with my life without even looking up and appreciating the beauty around me. Busy, preoccupied, or distracted, I miss the moment and lose out on all the wonderful feelings and memories that come with it. When it's time for me to look back The Rocking Chair Test, I want to remember the deep dinner conversations, the mist falling on my skin on that cool beach day, drives with the top down, music memories, the bubble bath that tickled my nose all night, the puppy I watched chase the birds round and round the park, getting a loving phone call the second I most needed it, stuffing a peanut-butter and jelly sandwich in my face in the impromptu winter fort (at the age of 32), speaking my truth when it felt so scary, and on… and on…

Now a peak life moment seeker, I am dedicated to finding more marvelous moments and mini life resting spots. When I make time for mini moments of reflection in ordinary spaces at home or work, I am more open to miracles out in the world.

Here are but few flairs that could transform ordinary experiences into extraordinary peak life moments:

- Turn a boring lunch salad into a 10-minute rejuvenating break outside.
- Have inspiring music or personal development CDs on stand-by when traffic comes to a screeching halt.
- Carry a journal or book with you everywhere you go. Have a spontaneous creative session that would have otherwise felt like a waste of time.
- Buy a gift card at the coffee shop and tuck it away in your wallet for a morning get-away surprise.
- Buy fresh flowers to greet you early Monday morning.
- Spray newly cleaned sheets with a lavender scent to help you sleep soundly and feel immense gratitude before you drift off.

Exercise

- Free your mind and play in daydreams of delight.
- Step into the present moment and stay there.
- Notice when you felt wonderful feelings in the past and seek out similar situations.

"Commitment unlocks the doors of imagination,
allows vision, and gives us the 'right stuff'
to turn our dreams into reality."

James Womack

Inner Garden Paradise

Play with me. Think outside the box and build a limitless mental retreat that you can visit any time you want. Visualize what your perfect safe haven would look like. Create it with your imagination. It can be an inviting physical space or just a mind-clearing space that doesn't require anything but a little quiet.

First find a place in your mind that feels clear, positive, whole, healthy, and relaxed. Give it physical elements such as gardens or rooms. Where can you see yourself happy and hanging out all day? Don't scrimp or save… you have all the money you need to build it to your exact specs.

How does it feel? What colors do you see? Is anyone else allowed there? Give limited access or set up boundaries if you like… add things or remodel anytime you want something different. Just erase, erase, erase, and create whatever you desire. Use all of your senses and bring your retreat to life!

Remember, it doesn't cost a dime to undergo major construction. It's your dream palace. Name it. Feel how connected you are to this private retreat. You are the only one who knows it exists. See how close it is for quick get-aways. You can pack up and take off instantly anytime you need a break. Sit quietly, brainstorm challenges or opportunities, offer some of your own expert advice, talk to yourself, relax, dance, play, or just hang – your inner garden paradise is yours for the taking.

Live, breathe, and feel how real this retreat is. It's always here in a nanosecond's notice.

Exercise

Build your own mental retreat and inner garden paradise…

- Have a room for physical therapy. Add any physical healing elements that you might want or need if your body is aching or weak today or in the future.

- Create a setting for meeting and sitting with people you love. Set up a special place that you invite others to come to when you want their company. They can listen, sit, or offer inspiring advice when you need it.

- Have a special place filled with energy. Anytime you need strength, courage, enthusiasm, verve, vitality, or positive energy take as much as you need from here. It constantly replenishes itself anytime you want, need, or desire it!

Sit, relax, and enjoy your inner garden paradise... any day, any time!

"Some things have to be believed to be seen."

Ralph Hodgson

Reveal Your Angels

Surround yourself with the most divine, lovely, and loving humans. Find people who love themselves enough to love you. Who support, cheer, and celebrate you! Who lift you and your spirits higher and higher.

When you are in good company you can do, breakthrough, and accomplish anything you desire. Have you ever been around someone who seemed to suck the life out of you? You almost always walked away feeling worse instead of better. Or maybe you just felt drained and depleted. I sometimes refer to these as "lower relationships." They can zap you of your power, passion, and purpose.

Then on the flip side there are the angels. The people who inspire you – you're attracted to their energy. They seem to see only the brilliance in you and encourage your continued success. You step away filled with energy, creativity, power, passion, and love – and feel like you could conquer anything.

Know the difference between the two types of people in your life. Create a circle of strength and energy. Live in a community of angels and say goodbye to some of the lower relationships that don't serve you at this time in your life. Make, find, and spend time with people who are uplifting.

Seek out the happy and successful people who are running ahead of you. Watch their stiletto strides and let them lead you on your happy journey!

Exercise

- Make a list of your current angels. Who supports and encourages you?
- Where could you find more positive people to surround you?
- Who else would you like to invite into your inner circle of angels?
- Who do you want to release and distance yourself from?
- How can you set up boundaries to promote the clear, clean energy of your angels and release the negative people you now know you need to steer clear of?

Be selective about your time and the company you keep. Allow the richness of wonderful women to flow into your life. Invite their input and listen to the lessons the most positive people you know have to share.

"In everyone's life, at some time, our inner fire goes out.
It is then burst into flame by an encounter with another human being.
We should all be thankful for those people
who rekindle the inner spirit."

Albert Schweitzer

Laws To Live By

- Focus on joyful possibilities.
- Know that you are loved and supported.
- Get rid of guilt.
- Don't compare yourself to others.
- Improve yourself instead of criticizing.
- Be accountable for your own actions.
- Be flexible.
- Be courageous.
- Be forgiving.
- View mistakes as an opportunity to learn what not to do.
- Be yourself.
- Be vulnerable.
- Find your purpose.
- Be in the moment.
- Feel at peace even when everyone else is in chaos.
- Share faith and hope.
- Control what you can and let go of what you can't.

"To freely bloom – that is my definition of success."

Gerry Spence

PLAY IS A STATE OF MIND

The Luxury Of Play

When is the last time you played? Or roared with laughter? When was the last time you let your hair down, put on your stilettos, and let loose? When did you last bathe in a delightful activity for the sole purpose of pleasure?

When was that again? Will you jot it down in your journal and remind me?

Don't think you could find another minute in the day to squeeze in play? Well, wouldn't you know it? The show-stopping stiletto version of your life says you don't have to make, find, or eek out one more second – but you can still play!

Play is a not a luxury. It's essential to living vibrantly and vitally. Look at all the benefits of play! They are as beneficial to your health as a deep tissue massage or yoga session… and cheaper!

Embrace the attitude of play. It's really more of a state of mind than an actual physical activity. It can be anything at all – anything that makes you smile or lets you imaginatively flitter through your reality for a moment. Work can even become "play" with the right attitude and a few quick tips.

Play

- *Brings joy and inner peace to your life.*
- *Fosters a sense of belonging and connection.*
- *Reduces stress.*
- *Promotes longevity.*
- *Inspires new thoughts and perspectives.*
- *Reduces conflict, stress, and worry.*
- *Restores optimism.*
- *Stimulates creativity.*
- *Renews your ability to accomplish and succeed.*
- *Encourages healthy risk taking.*
- *Opens the essence of who you are.*
- *Softens the heart.*
- *Heals wounds.*

Everyone plays differently. That's why there are over 400 play options from snoozing to sweating, and everything in-between. And I have no doubt by now that every one of these ideas will lead to many more fantastic brainstorms. Be unlimited in your play plans. Pick one – or pick all but one. Grab your journal now and let your imagination run wild. Write all the fun, silly, and relaxing things that come to mind. Then embrace a moment each day to enjoy time in play.

It's not the quantity of time you spend, but the quality of your delightful and playful intention.

Exercise

- Buy yourself gold stars and give yourself a shiny star every time you step outside of your comfort zone and attempt to play.
- Get a play buddy to share stories and laughs with at the end of each day.
- Start a "Play Guide" where you write down all your favorite play ideas and how you will make them uniquely yours.

> *"We don't stop playing because we grow old;*
> *we grow old because we stop playing."*

George Bernard Shaw

13 Play Principles

While you and I may enjoy life in very different ways, much of what we experience while in play transcends space and time.

Play:

- Lifts your spirit.
- Is transcendent.
- Is timeless.
- Comes naturally.
- Absorbs you in the moment.
- Transforms your energy.
- Brings balance to your life.
- Encourages spontaneity.
- Stops efficiency for the moment.

- Washes insecurity and anxiety away.
- Has no judgments.
- Has no right or wrong.
- Puts you in touch with yourself.

> *"You can discover more about a person in an hour of play than in a year of conversation."*
>
> Plato

Suggestions For 'Serious' Play

It's play time: the ultimate in NO rules! Just 17 simple suggestions to make every moment of play positively blissful.

- Make up your own rules.
- Shake up your routine.
- Take off your watch.
- Give 100% of your attention to the activity.
- Let go of the outcome.
- Slow down.
- Empty your mind.
- Savor the moment.
- Surrender to the experience.
- Don't take yourself too seriously.
- Stop keeping score.
- Get caught up in emotion.
- Take a leap into the unknown.
- Let surprises surface.
- Indulge yourself.
- Nurture your hobbies.
- Soak in the sunshine.

> *"Sometimes you have to play a long time to be able to play like yourself."*
>
> Miles Davis

Learn From A Child

Why is it that we grow up, become adults, and completely forget how to play? Take advice from Cherie Kerr and learn your lessons from the people who invented play. Watch children.

- Listen to their banter.
- Watch their free movements.
- See them become the experience of play.
- Watch which toys they select.
- Solve challenging problems.
- Entertain themselves.
- Use repetition or create patterns.
- Listen to the change in tone, tempo, and voice volume.
- Reveal opportunities you never knew existed.
- Transform into multiple characters on a whim.
- Make up stories, characters, names, and creatures.
- Perform in the school play.
- Transport themselves to another time and place.
- Bond with a stuffed animal.
- Enjoy the entertainment of playing with Tupperware®.
- Read a book.
- Pretend to be an adult.
- Make sense of the world.
- Discover something new.
- Chase their shadow.
- Skip the cracks in the pavement.
- Role play.
- Recount an experience.
- Build some structure.
- Respond to color and outside sensory input.
- Play hide and seek and find something that has been lost.
- Make funny faces.
- Take in their surrounding environment.

- Play with others.
- Interact with big kids or adults.
- Look at themselves in a mirror.
- Be silly… or be anything.

Be a Super Ball. Sometimes I pretend I can bounce, fly, swing, pounce, and rebound off anything. I blow off steam by pretending I'm a human super ball.

> *"There are no seven wonders of the world*
> *in the eyes of a child. There are seven million."*

Walt Streightiff

Paper, Pens, Pencils, And Play

Temporarily release yourself from responsibility. Relax and let words flow from your mind, through your hands, straight to your journal. Studies around writing therapy benefits have shown that when people write about difficult events for 20 minutes a day for three or four days, the function of their immune system improves.

- Journal early and often (I think you get a star here!).
- Count your blessings.
- Write short-term and long-term goals.
- Record your memories.
- Make a life list of things you want to do and accomplish.
- Write thoughtful notes with colorful and wacky pens.
- Create a simple poem.
- Log daily events you enjoyed.
- Write a children's book.
- Buy a calendar and write your feelings every morning.
- Hide notes around the house.
- Leave notes on your friends', family's, or spouse's car.
- Sneak a note into someone's briefcase, bag, or pocket.
- Use a dry erase pen on the bathroom mirror.
- Share inspiring words of wisdom.

- Get a pen pal.
- Keep a dream journal by your bed.
- Write a screenplay.
- Make up a humorous top ten list.
- Send a personal e-card (p.s. don't forward emails).
- Pick your favorite quotations and send them in blank cards on special occasions.
- Write a living will.
- Stay present and take notes when you are talking on the phone.
- Recycle greeting cards by keeping the front and tearing off the back. Use them as beautiful scratch paper or for love notes.
- Create a cartoon with captions.
- Write affirmations everywhere you want to see them.
- Drop personal thank-you notes in the mail anytime you are inspired.
- Buy lovely stationary and interesting paper you love to touch.
- Sign the inside of books you give as gifts.
- Brainstorm new ideas and don't let your pen stop.
- Write a nursery rhyme.
- Keep extra pens with you in case you want to give them away.
- Write love notes on your body with body-art crayons.
- Send a friend your personal book review.
- Caption your photos.
- Scribble nonsense words.
- Make up a new set of Ten Commandments you'd like to live by.
- Write down your thoughts and opinions.
- Get some of the feelings you rarely talk about out on paper (burn it later if you like).

Write a Children's Book. See the brilliant children's book *The Wooodles, Stretching Your Imagination* written by my dear friend Perla Fox. Almost ten years ago at the youthful age of 65, she embarked on her first book publishing adventure.

"Fill your paper with the breathings of your heart."

William Wordsworth

Soak In The Good Life

Relax a little. Pay attention to all the small things that make your life wonderful. Heighten your senses and let them out to play. Return to a time of simple pleasures where the smell of rain and freshly baked bread was almost miraculous.

- Pay close attention to scents that soothe you.
- Listen for sounds you love.
- Hear the rhythm in sizzling butter.
- Envision a beautiful garden and flowers with your eyes closed.
- Hear the crackling of a natural wood fireplace.
- Burn white sage and use it to cleanse your mind.
- Lather your body with chocolate massage butter lotion.
- Enjoy the smell of fresh roasted coffee and beans.
- Stop when you pass photos or art you love.
- Here the crackle of the ice cubes when you pour a glass of ice tea.
- Feel the breeze on your skin.
- Listen for the birds in the morning.
- Say your prayers.
- Use essential oils.
- Love your pet and be kind to animals.
- Listen intently to the world around you.
- Wear a tiara and be a princess for the day.
- Feel the dew on your skin when you are close to the ocean.
- Pretend your neighborhood is a foreign country.
- Smell fresh cut lemon, lime, or orange on your hands.
- Pick the petals off a flower, one by one.
- Care for the Earth's resources.
- Spray your sheets with a soft lavender scent.
- Enjoy the smell of a freshly mowed lawn.
- Wish on a star.
- Set the table with garden-picked flowers and candles.
- Say grace holding hands at the dinner table.
- Wear all the colors you normally wouldn't think go together.
- Drop a path of bread crumbs behind you.

- Wear your hair in pigtails.
- Make a serenity basket with some of your favorite things.
- Garnish your breakfast with sprigs of mint.
- Take your lunch in a kid's lunch pail.
- Turn off the television.
- Call your best friend and wear matching shirts across the miles.
- Appreciate your health every time you hear the sirens of an ambulance.
- Turn off the radio in the car and be with your thoughts.
- Smell and appreciate the energy of money the abundance of your life.

Daily Rituals. Use simple and relaxing rituals to restore your mind and body. The benefits of mini rituals are more colored by your intention and focus than any physical elements you choose to incorporate. When I have a situation that is particularly stressful or worrisome, I use a rock ritual. I write the concern on the back of the rock and set it next to a candle. I visualize the candle burning away the energy and feel a sense of peace knowing the universe is taking care of the situation in a much bigger and better way than I could.

"Nothing is worth more than this day."

Johann Wolfgang von Goethe

Slow Down And Self Care

Take in a deep breath.

Close your eyes.

Let go of the tension in your shoulders.

Feel the energy at the top of your head flowing down your neck and the muscles in your back. Let your limbs relax. Arms. Elbows. Wrists. Legs. Feet. Now…

s l o w l y

Feel the energy flowing through your fingers and toes. Your back deeply relaxing. Letting go… the tension melting… your eyes and face softening. Release your tongue from the roof of your mouth. Open your mouth wide and gently close your lips. Feel your jaw relax. Take another deep breath through your nose and exhale. Continue this wonderful meditative state or try:

- Yoga.
- A candle meditation.
- Calming breathing exercise. (5-count inhale. 5-count hold. 10-count exhale.)
- Gently swing on a bench or rocking chair.
- Put your head back and cover your eyes with a lavender eye pillow.
- Surround yourself with natural beauty.
- Listen to the relaxing sounds of water.
- Eat ceremoniously and welcome the benefits and pleasure of your food.
- Take a long bath.
- Daydream.
- Give yourself a foot massage.
- Find some alone time.
- Visualization to manifest what you desire in your life.
- Connect with someone who is kind and loving.
- Let your mind wander into a fantasy world.
- Spray refreshing mineral water on your face.
- Light candles.
- Try acupuncture.
- Use aromatherapy to inspire your moods.
- Breathe in the essence of life.
- See empty white space.
- Feel positive energy flowing through your body.
- Have your chakras aligned.
- Feel your affirmations deeply in your heart and belly.
- Send healing energy to your body.
- Visualize your heart sending and receiving love.
- Look for mini miracles throughout the day.

Schedule a Personal Rendezvous. Deborah schedules a date with herself once every three or so months. She locks herself in the house and has a three-hour date filling the house with music, smells, and experiences she loves. She may just burn aromatherapy oils, stay in bed with a book, and never leave; draw a bubble bath and line the bathroom with dozens of tea light candles; hire a massage therapist to come to the house; or give herself a facial and plop herself down on the couch for a silly mindless movie night and a box of Milk Duds.

"Woman loves company even if it is only
that of a small burning candle."

Georg Christoph Lichtenberg

Nourish Your Mind

The joy of learning is unsurpassable. Lose yourself in a new skill, idea, or creative outlet. You will feel so proud of yourself… you'll feel so attractive inside when you continually better and grow yourself. It doesn't have to be serious or boring. Learn a new sport, embrace a new trend or lifestyle interest, or dig into any topic that could change your life: personal development, business expertise, fashion design, international cuisine, or travel!

- Learn how to develop your own black and white photos.
- Study the psychology of color.
- Interview a landscape architect.
- Read inspiring literature.
- Learn how to roll sushi and eat with chopsticks.
- Study an extinct animal.
- Reread the classics.
- Subscribe to a cutting-edge magazine (Dwell, Futurist Magazine, FAST Company, Gourmet, Architectural Digest).
- Learn how to read music.
- Learn calligraphy.
- Attend an inspiring lecture.
- Learn how to professionally bid at an auction.
- Learn how to be a wine connoisseur.
- Join an astronomy club.
- Get a foreign language tutor.
- Trade books you've already read for new ones.

- Listen to personal development CDs while on the road.
- Join Toastmasters.
- Learn a craft like knitting, quilting, crocheting, or needlepoint.
- Take a course in miracles.
- Buy, sell, or trade used books.
- Experiment with a kid's science kit.
- Learn the art of communication.
- Map out the feng shui of your house.
- Study the game of chess from an outdoor tournament.
- Learn from your mistakes.
- Talk to any professional in a uniform about their job.
- Visit the arboretum and learn the names of trees, plants, and shrubs.

Get a Study Buddy. Grab a friend and go to the library. Pretend you are back in school. Take a back-pack and your journal and sit on the floor in awe while you surround yourself with hundreds of thousands of experiences, words, and wisdom.

> *"Get over the idea that only children*
> *should spend their time in study.*
> *Be a student so long as you still have something to learn,*
> *and this will mean all your life."*

Henry L. Doherty

Music Feeds Your Soul

Music isn't just beneficial to your health and happiness, it is magical. It can create an emotional shift in your feelings and attitude... immediately. Music expresses what words cannot. It is a "supra-sense" of sorts because it incorporates all your senses, feelings, and memories. On the surface music may seem to be a series of sounds, but it evokes life.

Real and powerful, it feeds your soul. It defines who you are... and redefines who you are at the same time. Tap into your many marvelous parts and see how the magic of music can transform you.

- Dance around the house and sing into your hair brush.
- Hum a tune.

- Sing in the shower.
- Whistle while you work.
- Try a tongue twister.
- Use special songs to strum the strings of your heart.
- Give someone a 'motor boat' on their belly.
- Go to a karaoke bar.
- Sing in the dark.
- Stay quiet for the day and let music be your primary form of self-expression.
- Listen to international music and awaken knowledge.
- Sing like the Chileans do at your next concert (every word at the top of your lungs)!
- Learn the words to an old classic.
- Soothe your soul with calming music when chaos surrounds.
- Call yourself and sing your favorite love song.
- Pretend you are the next "American Idol."
- Sing a song and get into the groove when you are performing a repetitive task.
- Sing your praises.
- Give yourself a signature song.
- Sing a story out loud and commit to the characters.
- Sing the musical scale.
- Put all of your favorite songs on one CD to sing along to in the car.
- Sing naked.
- Hear the musical rhythms in the Earth's silence.
- Leave musical voice messages.
- Make your own instrument or drum.
- Sing every friend Happy Birthday when you call.

Sing Happy Birthday. Stephanie got so many different and wonderful birthday calls one year she transferred the songs to her computer and made a birthday CD to celebrate her life and authentic self.

"Music is well said to be the speech of angels."

Thomas Carlyle

Play With People

Surround yourself with fabulous friends, and on the days you are the only one with you… be your own best friend!

- Solicit your friends' input on important decisions or changes you are going through.
- Communicate regularly and return calls.
- Support friends and attend their events and important invites.
- Share funny things that make you laugh.
- Talk about what's on your mind.
- Do something special to show a friend how reliable and committed you are.
- Make up your mind to air out any conflicts.
- Share your opinions, feelings, and preferences.
- Show gratitude for the people in your life.
- Convince someone to take a risk doing something they love.
- Don't interrupt.
- Remember important dates.
- Be a mirror and let others see their truth.
- Allow people you care about to express and discover their own passions.
- Give people room to make their own mistakes and learn from them.
- Learn the facts before you judge.
- Don't blame others.
- Compliment before you criticize.
- Stay present in your conversations with others.
- Collaborate your talents.
- Be a team player.
- Tell anyone and everyone you know how much you value them.
- Create healthy boundaries, but breakdown fear-induced walls.
- Invest in your relationships.
- Show up and show how much you care.
- Say, "I love you."

Visit www.shesite.com. Streaming genuine happiness in your life today… and everyday!   123

- Make and keep your promises – or just say no.
- Let honesty be your best policy.
- Give people the benefit of the doubt.
- Talk to strangers.
- Use smiles and hugs often.
- Make eye contact.
- Let go of the little things or find something humorous about them.
- Don't compare yourself to others.
- Enjoy a world of supportive women.
- Live abundantly and share your friendship, knowledge, and time like you have too much.
- Float in your creative dreams and see where they take you.
- Be curious about others and listen more than you speak.
- Ask about others' accomplishments.
- Speak words of encouragement.
- Use your intelligence and creativity to benefit others.
- Sing someone's praises.
- Visualize positive outcomes for the people in your life.
- Eliminate all "I told you so" comments.
- Celebrate the success of others.
- Inspire others to dream and achieve.

Dream Date. Take someone on a dream date that won't cost you a dime. The only topic of conversation is to share your dreams. Talk about what you love. Listen to what they want to do before they leave the planet. Hear what they want to accomplish and learn. Share wonderful places you'd like to travel to, the people you most admire, and the things you desire to have someday. Take notes so you can later give the person a written copy of their dreams so you can help them come true.

> *"Let us be grateful to people who make us happy,*
> *they are the charming gardeners*
> *who make our souls blossom."*

Marcel Proust

Totally Virtuous

You don't need an invitation to give to others. Make extraordinary acts of grace part of your life whenever it suits you. Be spontaneous and as you approach some of the more hectic times in your life, relax a bit. When you are a thoughtful friend year round, you can feel free and joyful during times that might otherwise feel obligatory and busy.

- Take a pan of lasagna to a friend who is under the weather.
- Help a friend with her grocery shopping.
- Volunteer to read to the kindergarten kids.
- Visit the residents at a local senior center.
- Take balloons to a Children's Hospital.
- Mentor someone in their business.
- Give your love generously.
- Show up with flowers for no reason.
- Let the people you love know you care with a personal note or call.
- Give your child a slightly longer hug before sending him off to school.
- Make breakfast in bed for someone you love.
- Tear out clippings, articles, or ideas your neighbor or co-worker might be interested in.
- Give someone a second chance.
- Lock your lips and throw the key away (just listen).
- Watch someone you love sleep.
- Leave an inspiring thought or quote on someone's voicemail.
- Record your favorite voice mails from children or special friends and give them back to them years later.

Give a Personalized Poem. Here's a little formula so you can write your own personalized poems and then share them while you reach out to people you love. Answer eight simple questions about who you are, what you love, and how you or others see you (or for the person you are writing it for). See the sample of mine at the end of the book if you want to use it as a guide.

1. Write your first name and all the nicknames you've been called or referred to in the past.

2. Write at least ten adjectives that describe you (if you think about some that start with the same letter, you'll add a bit of extra pizzazz).

3. Describe three important relationships or roles in your life that you play. Example: Mother of _____ (name of one child); Peacemaker of _____ (situation or place); Employee of _____ ; Friend of _____ ; Creator of _____ ; Lover of _____ ; etc…

4. List ten things that you love.

5. Five things you want to see.

6. Ten things you strongly dislike.

7. Where you currently reside (mentally or emotionally) or what occupies your mind. It can also be the physical place where you live, the time, day, hour, or era but you'll have to adapt the last line a bit. Think more along the lines of concepts that you believe in. Write three.

8. Your last name (or last nickname if you prefer).

Template For Joy Poem.

Title of Poem: **The Joy of** _____ (reside from # 7 or a nickname)

_____(1 adjective from # 2) _____(first name/s)…

_____, _____, _____, _____(4 adjectives from # 2)

_____ of _____ (an important relationship or role #3)

who loves _____, _____ and _____ (list 3 things you love from #4)

and dreams of _____, _____and _____(3 things you want to see from #5)

yet shies away from _____, _____and ___(list 3 things you dislike from #6)

she's one _____(1 adjective from #2) girl that ____(first name) _____(last name), living in a world of_____(write where you currently reside from #7).

"You give but little when you give of your possessions.
It is when you give of yourself that you truly give."

Kahlil Gibran, The Prophet

Color Me Brilliant

Use color to incite a silly smile, surprise, and sunbeam in an otherwise dreary day. Color evokes emotion and colors you wear all day will be absorbed into your body. Pull different colors into your day to calm your mind, give you a bit of oomph, create balance, open up your intuition, or encourage love and harmony.

- **Purple** is the color of royalty, spirituality, dignity, and sophistication. It can feel luxurious. Wear purple when you are meditating or any time you want to calm your body and mind.

- **Indigo** is the color to wear when you want to open up your intuition. The color of divine knowledge and the higher mind, wear indigo during your studies or quiet contemplative time.

- **Blue** instills a sense of belonging and trust, reliability, coolness, peacefulness, tranquility, security, faithfulness, and dignity. By far the most common 'favorite' color, wear blue when you have a need for heightened communication.

- **Green** depending on the shade can bring to mind nature, healing, freshness, growth, balance, compassion, abundance, money, and freedom. It is the easiest on the eyes and may have a therapeutic effect in stressful times.

- **Yellow** is most often associated with warmth, sunshine, and happiness. Wearing yellow will improve your ability to interact with the world and promote confidence and alertness.

- **Orange** creates a feeling of life-force energy, playfulness, pleasure, warmth and joyousness and is seen as vibrant and ambitious. Wear orange to spark creativity or when you go out to play. It's the color of fun!

- **Red** elicits the strongest emotional reaction, either positive or negative. It brings up feelings of love, passion, excitement, and strength, as well as those of anger, speed, and danger. Wear red to excite your emotions and show off your vibrant personality or feel simply sensual in your high heels!

- **Pink** is soft, sweet, and feminine and may elicit feelings of being nurtured or pampered. Wear pink on a date to encourage unconditional love in your heart or dissolve anger.

- **White** contains all the colors. It emphasizes purity, innocence, cleanliness, and spiritual development. Wear white when you want to illuminate your thought process and bring about clarity.

- **Black** most often represents sophistication and elegance. It can be seen as seductive, mysterious, or serious. Wearing black may give you the mental space for reflection and inner searching.
- **Brown** is earthy, solid, reliable, and effective. It grounds, stabilizes, and neutralizes. Wear brown when you are overexcited, need grounding, or seek a sense of healing.

Color Your Day. Copy this page and color your life brilliant. Tape it to the inside of your closet and use it anytime you want to stir certain emotions. If you need an energy boost, some power in your day, or something that will help you chill and relax – look to the color chart for inspiration and grab a sweater that will induce those emotions all day long.

"When in doubt, wear red."

Bill Blass

Let's Get Physical

Move your body to stir, shout, and feel the energy of life.

- Run barefoot.
- Learn the trapeze.
- Try gymnastics.
- Make up your own interpretive dance.
- Pretend you are a super ball and bounce off the walls.
- Do cartwheels and somersaults.
- Ride a bike.
- Play Frisbee.
- Learn to walk on stilts.
- Take a self-defense course.
- Take a long walk or go for a hike.
- Learn some groovy new dance moves.
- Jump on a trampoline.
- Learn a new sport.
- Move your furniture in a new design.
- Go indoor rock-climbing.
- Let your foot tap to the beat of the music.

- Flitter like a butterfly.
- Work up an appetite.
- Hula-hoop.
- Play ball and catch.
- Skip around the block.
- Boogie to the beat.
- Go horseback riding.
- Give a friend a piggy back ride.

Decadence Day. When was the last time you spent almost an entire day outside? Plan activities or extra time to lounge around outside from morning until night. Let go of any work concerns, e-mails, phone calls, to-do lists or responsibilities. Even though a decadence day doesn't have to be outside, there is one rule. Terri Levine says it is a 24 hour day without any work thoughts, conversations, or responsibilities. Be decadent and do exactly what you desire.

"The body says what words cannot."

Martha Graham

The Great Outdoors

Keep your body active and alive. Find serenity, pleasure, and adventure exploring the great outdoors.

- Make a special date to the watch the pinks and golds of the sunset.
- Pick wild flowers.
- Lay in the grass and name the shapes in the clouds.
- Start an ant or a worm farm.
- Play hop scotch.
- Run through the sprinklers.
- Climb a tree.
- Go bird watching.
- Feel the wind on your face.
- Visit a new neighborhood nearby.
- Play tag.
- Collect seashells.

- Catch tadpoles.
- Plant your favorite flowers in the garden.
- Have a snowball fight.
- Shape a topiary.
- Sit on rocks that have been warmed by the sun.
- Fly a kite.
- Name a star.
- Build a sand castle.
- Make a snow angel.
- Go on a nature walk.
- Stop to smell the roses.
- Visit a garden oasis or a nursery.
- Take a picnic to the beach.
- Flop in a hammock.
- Have a water balloon fight.
- Float in the pool until your toes prune up.
- Throw pennies in a fountain and make a wish.

Bird Watching. Priscilla sits and watches birds for hours on end. You would love her stories. Her eyes light up when she talks about how they always appear in her yard in pairs and sing uplifting songs of delight.

"Climb the mountains and get their good tidings.
Nature's peace will flow into you as sunshine flows into trees.
The winds will blow their own freshness into you, and the storms their energy,
while cares will drop off like autumn leaves."

John Muir

Wildly Creative

Live outrageously! Creatively express yourself. Surround yourself with color, textures, ideas, hobbies, patterns, and activities you love. Take life less seriously and be more creative.

- Patch old jeans into a funky new style.
- Make sock or finger puppets.
- Sponge paint a room in the house.
- Make bookmarks (iron crayon shavings between two pieces of wax paper).
- Press flowers or dry leaves to make a greeting card.
- Make refrigerator magnets from magnetic strips you can find at craft stores.
- Buy a kit to make your own candles or use a sheet of beeswax.
- Make a book about you. (Keep clippings of colors, ideas, dreams, pictures, and quotes that inspire you in a three ring binder).
- Make fresh scented potpourri bags for your closet or underwear drawer.
- Make chocolate, white chocolate, or peanut-butter spoons and enjoy with a weekend latte. Just melt chips in the microwave and dip plastic spoons into the chocolate, generously covering the spoon.
- Wrap presents with the Sunday comic pages.
- Make up a game.
- Make an encourage-mint jar to use as needed (Write words of inspiration on plain mailing labels and stick them on Andes® Chocolate Mints).
- Make a flower pen by wrapping green floral tape around a pen and the stem of an artificial flower.
- Make heart shaped glycerin soaps.
- Put some old photos in a scrapbook.
- Sew a scented pillow.
- Photo essay your day.
- Chart your family tree.
- Make a paperweight (Find a smooth stone and write an affirmation on it with a silver or gold metallic pen.).
- Color with Crayolas.
- Learn to draw on an Etch-A-Sketch.
- Play with watercolors.

Art Ahoy. Sign up for a local art class or something creative. Grab a friend who is interested, too. Marvel at the differences of your unique personalities that create a very distinctive piece from the same exact class and experience.

> *"Creativity represents a miraculous coming together*
> *of the uninhibited energy of the child*
> *with its apparent opposite and enemy, the sense*
> *of order imposed on the disciplined adult intelligence."*

Norman Podhoretz

Fun, Frivolous Things to Do

- Chart your happiness every morning.
- Take a model home tour.
- Make a reading list.
- Take the day off and do nothing.
- Give yourself a theme song.
- Make a "dream list" of things to do.
- Have a festive picnic.
- Test-drive a new car.
- Lollygag and loiter.
- Visit a pet store.
- Check out an art gallery.
- Innocently eavesdrop on a conversation filled with laughter.
- Shop in a toy store.
- Keep a slinky at your desk.
- Write in a rainbow of colors.
- Put stickers on your personal phone messages.
- Plan a scavenger hunt.
- Explore nature and bend down to smell the flowers.
- Plant your favorite fruit tree (or keep it in a large container on the patio).
- Get a 10-minute massage at the Farmer's Market.
- Chew gum and blow bubbles.
- Wander through a museum.

- Take your mind on a walk.
- Read and believe a new affirmation everyday.
- Use your senses – think back to the smell of real Xerox copies in grade school.
- Listen to books on tape.
- Play hide-and-go-seek.
- Listen to a children's CD "Schoolhouse Rock."
- Feel the beat of international music even if you don't understand the words.
- Blow bubbles.
- Build a fort.
- Play with a puppy.
- Get instant gratification and take pictures with a mini Polaroid.
- Play cards.
- Go shopping at the $.99 store and buy yourself a toy.
- Create a work of art on the sidewalk with chalk.
- Bang on a drum.
- Buy red shoes.
- Paint your toes a silly color.
- Write "I ♥ Me!" in permanent marker on your old panties.
- Play dress up (or dress down for the day if you are always formally dressed).
- Drink hot chocolate with marshmallows.
- Strike a pose or pretend you are a robot.

Make a Rainstick. Barbara created a rainstick to calm and center her students as they would arrive for yoga. She sealed one end of a cardboard tube and hammered nails into the tube to create a maze inside. Be creative and decorate the outside. Look for special pebbles, corn kernels, and seeds to drop into the tube to create a "raindrop" noise to soothe you.

> *"I still get wildly enthusiastic about little things…*
> *I play with leaves.*
> *I skip down the street and run against the wind."*

Leo F. Buscaglia

Visit www.shesite.com. Streaming genuine happiness in your life today... and everyday!

133

Snooze To Slumber

Make the very last moments of your day special. How you fall asleep directly corresponds to how you feel when you wake. Every night before you retire make sleep tight wishes and give bedtime kisses.

- Make your bedroom a sleep sanctuary.
- Let someone tuck you in.
- Get and give soft kisses.
- Take a warm bath.
- Drink herbal tea (chamomile is relaxing).
- Think relaxing thoughts.
- Listen to meditation tapes.
- Keep the lights dim before you go to bed.
- Wear something ultra wonderful and comfortable.
- Sleep on 600-plus thread count cotton sheets.
- Read inspiring short stories.
- Set your bedroom to the ideal sleep temperature (60–65 degrees Fahrenheit).
- Pull the covers up to your chin.
- Close your eyes in time to get a full eight hours of sleep.
- Soundproof your room.
- Install an automatic thermostat so you can crawl in and out of bed while its warm.
- Use affirmations so you will wake up on the right side of the bed.
- Crawl into clean sheets.
- Decorate your pillowcase or write an affirmation in a permanent marker.
- Hug someone late before bed and first thing early in the morning.
- Rest when you are tired.
- Count your blessings like sheep before you sleep at night.
- Celebrate your daily ah-has and accomplishments every night before you go to bed.

Tuck Yourself In. Check in early one night a week and crawl in bed with a good book, audio CD, or sketch pad. Enjoy the quiet of your mind and knowing of your soul.

> *"I have always been delighted at the prospect of a new day,*
> *a fresh try, one more start, with perhaps a bit of magic*
> *waiting somewhere behind the morning."*

J.B. Priestly

Bon Appetite

Prepare to dine. Either pick up the biggest piece of chocolate you can find or mix and match these ingredients to create your own delectable masterpiece. I have a sneaky suspicion that you have every ingredient you need right there in your girlish cupboards.

- Pinch of gratitude.
- Liter of vision.
- Spoonful of spunk.
- Smidgen of organization.
- Bushel of optimism.
- Cup full of confidence.
- Plenty of friends.
- Splash of connection.
- Pound of truth.
- Pints of personal promises.
- Can of compassion.
- Bucket of grace.
- Dashes of joy.
- Demi of love.
- Drops of kindness.
- Fifth of authenticity.
- Gallon of giggles.

- Peck of persistence.
- Quart of goodness.
- Shots of affirmations.
- Teaspoon of preparation.
- Heaping spoonfuls of faith.
- Barrel of inspiration.
- And, floor yourself with tons of fun.

Open yourself up to a continual playful state of mind. Do something courageous, fun, and frivolous every day. It doesn't have to be big. Tap into your creativity, feel your stress lesson, and your spirit soar as you soak in the joy of play and the sound of your own giggles.

> *"A little work, a little play,*
> *To keep us going – and so, good day!"*

George Du Maurier

SUMMARY: STRUT YOUR STUFF

You Are Not Alone

Girl, when you live it… when you own the woman you are… the most wow stuff shows up! You show up. It's beautiful and incredible!

The core of your happiness lies in your self-knowledge.

Contemplate and meditate about who you are. Ask good questions and open yourself up to answers that will enlighten, surprise, and delight you… and the sketchy ones might even entertain you. It's all part of the wonderful discovery process.

I believe the scariest parts of me are the parts I don't know. Don't be afraid to ask yourself tough questions. Your truth will shine through. Look at all those pages of truth in your journal right now. You clearly seek a deeper level of self-knowledge and expression! Be sure you continue your journey.

You are not alone. Other women are right here with you – in this very moment. They understand because they have been through your experience. I know it feels like you must be the only one… but you are not alone. I guarantee you someone else knows exactly what your situation feels like.

- Connect with others.
- Get support.
- Find a buddy.

Ask people you trust to share their lessons. Learn from their experience. And seek knowledge from people in all different walks of life and with different levels of education, an opposite view, or completely different passion. See the many options in the world and keep making choices that fit and are right for you!

- Continue to have conversations with people you trust so you learn more about yourself at the deepest possible level.
- Gain deep knowledge about who you are by taking small risks and putting yourself in new situations.
- Get a crew of angels to support you and celebrate the choices you make and successes you achieve!

If you are even slightly interested in meeting another woman in your area or by phone that is also going through the *Shout From The Rooftops In Your Stilettos* process, send me a quick email now. Your angel might be sending over an email at the exact same time. Calling all Stiletto Angels at www.shesite.com.

> *"We can all be angels to one another. We can choose to obey*
> *the still small stirring within, the little whisper that says,*
> *'Go. Ask. Reach out. Be an answer to someone's plea. You have a part to play.*
> *Have faith.' We can decide to risk... the world will be a better place for it."*
>
> Joan Wester Anderson

A Recap Of Extreme Happiness And Self Knowledge

- Watch all the changes that take place in your heart, mind, and body throughout the day.
- Get in touch with your feelings, thoughts, and emotions so you can deepen your self knowledge.
- Watch your thoughts pass through your mind without analyzing, assessing, commenting, or judging them.
- Be aware of the detail of life around you.
- Talk through your thoughts and opinions with someone you trust.
- Take a step back whenever possible and view yourself as an outsider would.
- Pretend today is your first day on Earth. Observe yourself as you see, hear, smell, touch, taste, and know in your heart all the newness around you.
- Keep your journal nearby and write down fun inspirations and repetitive or recurring thoughts. Look for patterns.
- Take responsibility for your thoughts and actions.
- Visualize your life as you want it to be.
- Watch the images, people, activities, and ideas you are attracted to. Spend time with them!
- Ask yourself, "What life lessons do I still want to learn?"
- See yourself as others see you.
- Take inventory of your day and think about what you are proud of and what would make it even better.
- When you go to bed, fall asleep asking yourself, "How can I joyfully get in touch with my true self?"

Wishing You Well In Your Saucy Stilettos

You've only got to do one thing... BE YOURSELF!

- Stand up tall and be proud of who you are, your gifts, and the value you add!
- Focus on your strengths. The more you love yourself, the more others will love you, too.
- Visualize your favorite traits in a big way (having fun, staying connected, and being interested and interesting) and you will exhibit more of them.
- Practice praise.
- Be kind to yourself when you make mistakes. Forgive yourself and move on.
- Expose yourself to positive people you enjoy and plan to be around them.
- Speak up and confidently express your thoughts when you have something to say.
- Do more of the things you love and are great at!

Deep down, I believe you have every answer, solution, and spark of inspiration you need to live an amazing, fulfilling, and happy life! Sometimes you know it...it just flows. But other times your oars get stuck in murky waters and you feel paralyzed or just too weak to paddle through.

I see your beauty – there's so much waiting to be unleashed! Every bit of what you desire is deep within you. Trust yourself. Make a choice to authentically and honestly live from a place of happiness. Let yourself be free, play, and enjoy all the simple pleasures of life.

I can't wait to look up and catch a glimpse of your brilliant smile and dazzling stilettos prancing on the rooftops.

> *"Care more than others think wise.*
> *Risk more than others think safe.*
> *Dream more than others think practical.*
> *Expect more than others think possible."*

Howard Schultz

The Joy of Julie

Bouncy Jooligan…

courageous, compassionate, confident, connected

creator of happiness and joy

who loves yoga, surprises, and lattes

and dreams of being surrounded by fresh flowers, an organized closet and impromptu dinner parties

yet shies away from knick knacks, cold air, and people who generally suck

she's one silly girl, that Jooligan Hunt,

living in a world of love and light.

Julie Hunt is a free flowing source of hope, energy and inspiration who tells it like it is giving straight forward and simple tips and advice so you can live happier days and obliterate the monotony of life. She is on a self propelled mission to scream, skip, run, jump, shout, dance, and sing with women all around the universe who want live a vivacious life busting at the seams!

A happiness-making machine, she's devoted to creating pure bliss in women's lives. She splashes streaming tips of happy essentials that are fun and easy to swallow, feel good about, and great to experience.

"Every day is a treasure — a gift from the universe
— so fill each day with more joy, smiles, brilliant fun and simple happy essentials."

Julie Hunt

Now, try on your stilettos and embrace the vibrant life that awaits you!